Employee Emotional Abuse

Oppressive Working Environments

Employee Emotional Abuse
Oppressive Working Environments

According to King David
"...He that rules over men [must] be just, ruling in the fear of God. And [he shall be] as the light of the morning, [when] the sun rises, [even] a morning without clouds; [as] the tender grass [springing] out of the earth by clear shining after rain" [II Samuel 23:3b-4] KJV.

B.Y. Stuart, MEd PhD LCPC

Employee Emotional Abuse
Oppressive Working Environments

Printed in the United States of America
ISBN-13: 978-1484197196

About the Author

Dr. Stuart is an ordained minister and Licensed Clinical Pastoral Counselor. She has written many inspirational books on various topics pertaining to the Christian experience. Including are books on marital relations and youth life. For more about her and other publications, go to www.frministry.org/

Table of Contents

Acknowledgements

Employee Emotional Abuse acknowledges those workers who have experienced the social crime of emotional abuse in the workplace. Crimes committed by ruthless, insensitive, brutal, and nefarious persons who are irresponsible and hateful, and yet are in leadership positions.

People who are despicable, unscrupulous, and devious in their behaviours often dispel their prejudices in the workplace in the form of abuse towards those whom they supervise.

Those persons administer cruelty and social violence causing embarrassment, shame, and humiliation to those who suffer.

Workplace emotional abuse is not limited to any particular type of work environment, but it seems more prevalent in the educational, and other service-oriented employment facilities.

The persons who issue emotional cruelty use verbal abuses, unfair yearly reviews, exploitation, and misuse of company policies to manipulate, hurt, and otherwise take advantage of unsuspecting workers who only want to express their sense of responsibility by providing for their families. Those persons work under severe pressures to keep their jobs.

Unfortunately, with the present economic unrests, there will be more abuses as employees work under the threat of a lay-off if only to hold on to a job.

The workplace is a place where employees respond to their responsibility to provide for their families.

However, the experiences of some workers have made what should have been a pleasant working environment to be one, which is frightening, and tenuous because of insensitive supervisors and managers.

What is Employee Emotional Abuse?

Employee emotional abuse is the systematic use of any form of *indignities* to *humiliate, manipulate, dominate, coerce, influence,* and *control* another person to conform to specific insensitive prescriptive behavioural patterns.

As the manipulation continues, the internal feeling of pain becomes intense and affects the individual psychologically, mentally, socially, and physiologically.

The individual who suffers then begins to build an *emotional structural mechanism of defense* to cope with the constant abuse of the emotions, self-esteem, self-worth, and self-confidence. That defense mechanism could be to repress or consciously ignore insults, threats, put down, and shame.

Barbara Stuart
2013

Employee Emotional Abuse

"Although employee abuse is not new, it has taken a new feature with an environment of unending and relentless pressure due to increased competition and ineffective strategies for increasing competitiveness" (Bassman, 1999, p.4).

Introduction

After working for several years in the nursing and teaching professions, as an employee in each field, there were many situations to face and issues to deal with. Even being able to control a noisy session in a classroom was not daunting so much as did some of the experiences encountered working as an Administrative employee in higher education.

Working at this high level of learning one expects advanced aesthetic behavioural patterns from deans, and professors. Sure, they are there in abundance. However, one figment of their makeup was lacking in many cases, and this was the use of common sense and sensitivity for other individuals. Apparently, the potential for finding a combination of intellect and common sense were missing. After the first year, those high expectations were quickly abandoned.

In contrast to the secondary school setting and working with colleagues, this was a respectful and decent relationship. There was free will in the expression of emotions, and in most cases, rank did not qualify or exclude anyone from being emotionally expressive with due professionalism. With the new settings, there was no respect for personal feelings and titles were outdated. This new culture was completely different from any previously known.

Moreover, the expectation of employees in the lower échelon was that they should merge into the décor and lose their identity. It did not take long to find out that all educational accomplishments were quickly submerged, and became unmentionables in the new settings. No one cared if you had an advanced degree while working in an entry-level position. The PhDs and MAs blended with the high-school dropouts at the support staff level.

What made matters worse is that people from certain ethnic backgrounds, became tokens in front desk positions, thus giving the public a false impression that *everyone* who applied for a job in the establishment is treated equally.

Truthfully, employees from certain ethnic backgrounds were for the most part, selected as make-up to meet national employment quota. Hidden from the public's knowledge is the fact that majority of employees from *those* cultures, remain in low-paid positions until retirement. A few might gain recognition for a higher position after decades of working at the support staff level.

In those situations, one finds many unhappy, frustrated, and angry workers. Each individual expects validation, and recognition. However, when desires are not accomplished there is tension in the atmosphere mixed with resentment and disharmony.

Every employee deserves respect, and the right to work in an emotionally healthy environment. Nevertheless, there are times when the working environment is not conducive either to maintain self-esteem or for building self-confidence.

Many factors will contribute to work-related issues, which will make the employee unhappy and dissatisfied with the working conditions.

While this writer did not carry out a systematic research for this book, there are personal experiences and vignettes from other workers who are working in or have worked in an emotionally destructive unhealthy environment.

Disappointingly, despite the incidence and reports of employee emotional abuses, it is very difficult to prove even through internal and especially external investigation.

Unlike physical and sexual abuses, emotional abuse leaves no visible evidence. Seemingly, only a professional therapist is able to detect the signs and evidence of emotional abuse.

Worker dissatisfaction arises from many situations such as the lack of opportunities for promotion and job enrichment. One of the main dissatisfactions employees are concerned about is job enrichment. Each person wants to know that there are opportunities for growth and development, to use judgments, solve problems, and working under one manager.

The evidence of dissatisfaction is usually the lack of employee recognition, loss of self-confidence, ostracism, dull routines, boredom, fatigue, unfair treatment, over-work, and micro management.

Furthermore, if management is not supportive in dealing with problems, interpersonal conflicts will exist among workers.

Since men have always had the leading role in the workplace, this book will refer to managers and supervisors as males, except in cases where reference is to a female for clarity.

Chapter 1   People and Work

The world of work has become one of the most important interests in the life of every person who has an ambition to be productive and independent. One could attest that working people spend more time on their jobs than in their homes. If we average the total hours from the time of waking and getting ready, plus travel, the hours at work and getting back to our homes we will find that a typical worker spends an average of 12-14 hours with work-related activities.

Since people spend so much time earning a living, each individual needs to be happy while on the job. This does not mean that employers will be able to provide all their employees' needs since there are obligations on both sides. Nevertheless, both employee and employer have needs each can provide for the other. Yet, there are times when the scales become unbalanced and someone suffers. Many workers are dissatisfied either with their working conditions, the management, or with other workers.

Despite those factors of dissatisfaction, the major issue which produce problems for employees is poor communication. If employees and management fail to communicate effectively, this results in low morale, poor performance, and high turnover.

With low morale, employees go to work because of their own personal needs. The job does not excite them and in most cases, there is no motivation, and many end up looking for ways out of their situation. In such a setting, it is usual to find that there are poor interpersonal relationships among the employees.

People go out to work for many reasons. Those could be general or personal. Some of those reasons include, to provide income for their families and themselves, to secure a comfortable financial retirement, for vacation, to buy a home, education for themselves and/or their children, and for financial independence.

Nonetheless, every employer who provides work for an employee should seek to make the experience as comfortable as possible. It is the employer's responsibility to maintain the correct temperature; fairness, provide adequate payment for work done; develop opportunities for job enrichment and advancement. They should also be insightful in the realization of employee's competencies; and give a fair reward for good performance.

For many people the workplace is the best opportunity to experience community. It becomes a second home for them. For them, the workplace is where they meet their friends, and socialize with one another. Therefore, those persons expect conditions satisfying to their needs.

The employer however, expects loyalty, honesty, and excellent work ethics from each employee. Despite this, although many workers co-operate over and beyond in some cases, various war stories bear record of some socially unsafe workplaces coupled with cruel and insensitive supervisors.

In addition, the unstable economic conditions of present day create many frightening situations that leave the average worker dizzy with fears. Those fears arise from the threat of sudden layoffs, surprised mergers, and corporate financial failures, which often lead to bankruptcies.

Nowadays, it is usual to hear of someone who has worked for decades in an organization, and who has to take early retirement making the individual suddenly unemployed, and maybe without a pension and medical insurance. Every employee faces some type of pressures in the workplace, and it is not getting better.

Chapter 2   Realities of the Working World

One of the realities in today's workplace is that the average employee must be able to think on his feet; deal with problems expeditiously; do multi-task activities, and with a readiness to accept changes without warning. To meet those demands, the employee must possess multiple competencies to generate high profits and keep the employer competitive and productive.

Furthermore, that individual must have a strong capacity to deal with stress. In fact, some job descriptions ask that the applicant be "able to deal with stress, and frequent interruptions." It is unfortunate to note that many employers seem oblivious to the feelings and welfare of their employees. Their main interest is to get the work done and increase in profits. Moreover, the technological advancement in today's workplace has made competition even more intense, so that employers are demanding more commitment from their employees. Added to the over-commitment of employees is the factor of employee abuse. In some instances, it is like flogging a horse with a lame leg to run harder, or for a greyhound to run beyond its physical capacity.

Take for example Mark, a 35 year old in a middle management position. He is single, and his job requires a certain amount of traveling. Although he knew this before joining the company, he did not expect to be a scapegoat each time someone was required to go out of town. According to him, "I no longer seem to have a life because I am now living out of a suitcase." "Most times I am away for three or four weeks at a time with only a respite of a weekend at home in between travels."

Listening to the individual, the evidence of anguish was noticeable along with stress, and frustration. Here is a case in point of an individual who is experiencing a veiled form of employee abuse. Admittedly, the factor of travel was in the job description, but there was no discussion about the frequency during the interview.

The above gives an illustration of the hidden realities, not noted in the job description at an interview. Understandably, there will be items the applicant will overlook, no matter how well prepared that person might be. For this reason, it is easy for the employer to disguise or gloss over some details in order to have a vacancy filled if everything else is in order. The applicant, who is desirous of securing a job, might inadvertently ignore pertinent questions in order to "get a foot into the door."

Similarly, at the time of an interview, the complete description of a job is often indirect, and the employer might subtly masks some details, until after the individual has completed the term of probation. Furthermore, some descriptions are extremely vague, almost like the privacy statements one receives these days from credit cards, and insurance companies.

Advancement in Technology

Another reality is that technology is advancing at an unprecedented speed, creating numerous types of employment resulting in continuous changes in the workplace. Furthermore, the development of newer jobs makes it necessary for an employee to keep up with trainings, which require multiple skills, high competencies, and qualifications suitable for more than one types of employment. Therefore, the contemporary college student must consider those factors when planning a career.

Importantly, that student must enter fields with greater opportunities of obtaining a viable position representing the educational ability, and any technical training received while in college. After college, some students have had to take further technical training in order to obtain a suitable position in the working world. In addition, students must know that a college degree only gives an entry-level position in most areas depending on the type of study and skills attained.

The realities are that while there may be a wide variety of vacancies in an institution or corporate establishment, it does not mean that first consideration will be for qualified vested employees. In many cases, even though individuals meet the academic qualifications for a particular position, the organization or institution often turns down their application for promotion to a higher level. A senior administrator told an employee: "there are people here with PhDs in support staff positions." In other words, "be satisfied with your job."

Employer Unreasonable Demands

There are times when the duties of a vacant position are included in another employee's responsibilities. This results in less people doing more work within the same time span each day, and without an increment in pay.

Although the employee must ensure that he performs adequately, those situations will impinge on the emotions and create added stress. In some situations, the employee may refuse to carry out duties not included in the contract at the time of employment, especially if that person is unionized. However, there are places where employers will deny workers the privilege of joining a union. The employees are then at the mercy of their employers.

Take for example Blake, a middle-age professional, who had another job merged with his other duties after over 10 years in the establishment. Although he protested, this did not help and he is still in the position because it is difficult to find a new position with similar pay.

Obviously, without warning the employer can change the job description in mid-air. Situations such as those create emotional problems, bitterness, malevolence, and hostilities. These are evidences of lack of respect towards an employee.

Chapter 3   Conditions of the Working Environment

The sudden threat of the loss of a job is one of the most devastating situations anyone will ever experience. The emotional impact is unimaginable, and each day seems unending after a lay-off. The loss of employment is not only a financial setback, but also an emotional wound to the individual who unexpectedly, is out of a job. To lose one's job without advanced warning will be similar to losing part of the self.

According to one individual,

> *"I was working at my desk one morning when someone told me that my job was posted. There was no notification before it happened. I recalled having an anxiety attack immediately. My body trembled as if it would not stop."*

Job Security

Job security is an expected need and vital to every employee when that person enters a place of employment. Still, job security often comes with a great price. If a supervisor uses intimidation, or fails to listen to employees' problems, this will influence the free flow of communication from employee to management. Furthermore, if the employees do not receive support from management, or there is insensitivity towards their needs, the need to keep their job will prevent them from seeking help or making reports even against a cruel supervisor.

Since many are seeking social fulfillment and stability in their jobs, they may be fearful of losing that position and starting all over again. Consequently, they will disregard emotional distress and infractions from inconsiderate supervisors. Unfortunately, when employees are in this situation it is usual for the violation of policies along with unfair rewards for good work, to go unnoticed if only to keep their jobs.

Friendly Atmosphere

All employees want to feel included in a warm and friendly atmosphere. They need surroundings favourable for cheerfulness, self-expression, and supportive feedback. Nevertheless, other factors will disturb the emotional well-being of the employee such as being un-informed of changes, delays, and new procedures. Furthermore, if the process of communication is weak or the circulation of information is not in a timely manner, there will be dissatisfaction and unhappiness.

Besides, the breakdown of communication frequently causes other problems resulting in disagreement between managers and employees. For example, if there is evidence of favouritisms the employees will become discourteous towards each other, thus making the atmosphere even more stressful and tense for everyone. In such a setting, employees will not be supportive when it comes to loyalty and taking care of materials and equipment.

Dissatisfaction breeds Carelessness

When there are feelings of dissatisfaction among employees, whatever the reasons, their attitudes will be negative. In their minds, no one cares about them and their efforts are meaningless other than the pay they receive for their work. Employees will also become emotional, and this reflects in their behaviour both psychologically and physiologically (Beehr, 1995). Dissatisfied employees will demonstrate some types of reaction when there are disturbances, which make them angry, sad, or unhappy.

Depending on how each individual evaluates the identified emotion, the behaviour will follow the outcome of the internal process. Occasionally an employee may complain about a supervisor, but this can become a discredit against that person since there are performance reports on each individual.

Those reports can affect future promotions and salary increases. These are reasons why employees are forced to work under severe emotional constraints despite their feelings of dissatisfaction with their employment position.

Unfair Treatment of Employees

Regrettably, many employers seem to be unaware of those factors which make an employee *want* to work, rather than *have* to work in their establishments. In places such as educational institutions, employees face a great deal of unreasonable expectations as "part of the job" on a daily basis. Apparently, those establishments seem to have unwritten laws for employees to accept insults from students as part of the usual occupational routine. For this reason, rather than express their feelings many employees have to restrain emotions, no matter how mild those responses might be.

Nevertheless, it is important for every individual to acknowledge emotions because they are central to the entire being. As described by Hochschild,[i] who stated that an emotion is a "biologically given sense" making it as important as any other senses that humans possess.

For instance, we feel cold when the temperature falls; we are surprised when approached unawares; and we differentiate sounds and smells. Those are all signals to which we respond. Emotions are indeed similar to those biological sensations. Moreover, it is from those stimuli we respond because emotions are the reaction to an event we encounter whether pleasant or unpleasant. A sweet smell will make us smile; but something stale will make us frown. Therefore, people at work need to be free to express themselves in a controlled manner. Why should an employee accept emotional abuse from a customer with a smile? Why should a worker accept insults and rudeness from managers, professors, and students without a tinge of displeasure?

Although someone should have the right to respond to abuse, this must be with professionalism and social decorum. To act or respond impulsively will create many problems, both for the individual and the organization. In addition, emotional signals are communicable to the onlooker. It is the evaluation of eye contact, our cheerfulness, friendliness, and our rebuke or aloofness, which indicates to others', "it is safe or not safe" to approach.

Conditions of the work environment can be either positive or negative. Those conditions are what will make an employee satisfied or dissatisfied. Depending on the needs of the employee, that person may consider the job only as a stepping-stone to reach a personal goal.

> I was employed in a high-tech corporation for three years. During that time, my supervisor harassed me with verbal attacks usually in the presence of my colleagues. I approached him to inform him of my feelings concerning the behaviour. After talking with him, this went unnoticed and the behaviour continued. I later, went to the senior manager and made another complaint with reference to my confrontation with the supervisor. The senior manager listened, at least this was what I thought, and promised that he would address the situation. I waited for months to have a feedback, but I heard nothing more. As expected, the behaviour did not stop. In the end, I was laid off.

In another example the boss instructed the employee to make misrepresentations for him to cover his own failures. The employee refused to carry out such demands, which resulted in threats, open derision, screams, put-downs, and name-calling. The employee, who has to work under such conditions without a defense is under great pressure trying to maintain personal dignity, professionalism, and character.

> *According to Lesley*: I was employed for over 3 years. In the last year, I received no bonus; I was not invited to meetings and as a member of a group, I was ostracized. I discovered that my immediate boss made a number of mistakes, which I corrected, but he received the commendation. I said nothing even though I spared him from open disgrace. This went on for a while. Eventually, he told me in the presence of others to "find another job." I was deeply hurt, and in a week, I was laid off. What was most sickening is that I was invited to the Christmas party. I did not turn up.

This report only synthesized researchers' findings of employers' insensitivities towards employees. Why would this person want to attend a party after the treatment received by this employer?

Abuses are often verbal which manifests itself in a variety of ways. For example, when a supervisor tells an employee, "you are a hopeless case," this cuts to the very core of the person's soul. It goes very deeply especially if the person is a reliable worker. Situations such as these will make the employee want to forget and for this reason, the individual will hide feelings if only to hold to the job.

Another incident occurred when the employer told the employee "your days are numbered" in the presence of others. The employee reported feeling embarrassed, but kept quiet rather than have a confrontation. In the end, this person also was laid off from work.

There are always two sides relating to an event. However, who listens to the side of the employee who is at the mercy of *cruel* educational institution and corporate organization *tyrants*?

Chapter 4   Factors Affecting Emotions

Our emotions are part of the make-up of the total self. If those emotions become unhealthy for whatever reasons, the individual suffers. Each day an employee will experience various types of forces from the work environment affecting the emotions. Those forces come from external and internal sources and in various ways including the following.

Blame

For example, if a supervisor gives an employee wrong instructions on how to carry out a project this will cause problems. If after discovering that the outcome was not what was expected and the supervisor puts the blame on the innocent employee, this will affect him/her both internally and externally. Internally, there is cognitive processing affecting the emotions resulting in negative feelings. Externally, the employee might respond with irritability or in anger. Below is a diagram showing the process of an emotional event.

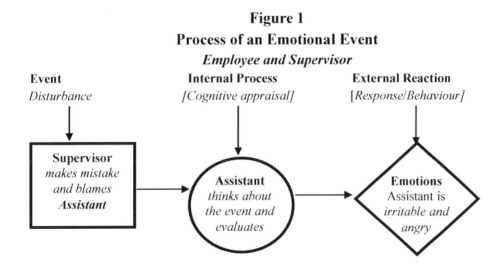

Figure 1
Process of an Emotional Event
Employee and Supervisor

Event	Internal Process	External Reaction
Disturbance	*[Cognitive appraisal]*	*[Response/Behaviour]*

Supervisor *makes mistake and blames* ***Assistant***

Assistant *thinks about the event and evaluates*

Emotions Assistant is *irritable and angry*

©2013 Diagram Adapted by B. Y. Stuart

After the event with the supervisor and employee, will the response be negative or positive? Will it be passive or active, covert or overt? Will someone be disappointed or pleased? Will a position be lost? The determination concerning the response will depend on the outcome of the employee's evaluation of the event.

There are occasions when situations occur with no time to filter and analyze the correct response. Actions can be very spontaneous depending on the emotional health and personality of the employee. For a situation such as blame, there will be tension due to the weight of the feelings of hurt from the effect of this negative situation. The individual may experience anxiety, frustration, pain, humiliation, sorrow, anger, or disappointment.

We cannot avoid those feelings resulting from negative emotional events in our lives. Nevertheless, employers expect the employee to control emotions regardless of the situation. They are unconcerned about the constant suppression of stressful feelings that will eventually result in psychological and physiological problems. Those problems are often communicable through the emotions, and this will create interpersonal conflicts. Still, most service establishments such as educational institutions seem to program their employees to conceal, smother, and repress their emotions for the benefit of maintaining goodwill from customers and clients, and for high productivity [*See endnote citation Hochschild, 1983*]. Therefore, it would be very unlikely for those employees to act out of character when problems arise.

Employee Exploitation

Many times employees are asked to work long hours with no compensation. One employee had to make personal calls for the employer, buy flowers, pay bills, and make excuses for a supervisor who was rarely present. This may sound incredible, but it is true.

Unfair Treatment

The occurrence of unfair treatment, coupled with financial inequities is prevalent where there are evidences of employee abuse. According to Hegtvedt (1990) "seeing oneself as unfairly treated indicates the lack of fulfillment of reward expectations and should lead to negative assessments and a general negative emotion, anger" (p.217).

She further noted that, "inequity affected respect, satisfaction, and anger more strongly than other emotions" (p.216). The evidence of unfairness will hurt an employee more than other situations. When there is unfairness from the employer, it indicates that the employee is inferior and undeserving of appreciation. The employee "may mask certain emotions because of the perceived risk associated with revealing them" (Johnson, Ford, & Kaufman, 2000, p.108). Anger is a very volatile emotion, which can result in destructive consequences if it is not controlled. The emotion can be a response reaction to unfair treatment of an employee inflicted by an insensitive supervisor.

Collette worked four years at a certain higher education institution. On one occasion, the supervisor wrote a negative report preventing her from receiving her yearly increment stating, "The department could not afford it." However, one week after that conversation, a new person was employed at the same level. Obviously, Collette was very angry, but dared not voice her opinion for fear of losing her job. Thus, the cycle of suppression of feelings, and employee abuse continued.

Poor Managerial Skills

The structure of all employment settings has various levels of supervision. However, many times those hired for the position of supervision, only possess intellectual abilities, but they do not have a clue about interpersonal relationships, dealing with emotional and conflict situations, and the management or supervision of others. *Those persons attack rather than correct, coerce rather than lead, and blame rather than teach.*

Seemingly, managers who lack interpersonal and conflict managerial skills are predisposed to being more troublesome and intractable when dealing with problems on the job. This is especially so, when they unleash their ineptitude on an undeserving employee. What is even more distressing is that those same incompetent persons write performance appraisals, which can be detrimental to the unsuspecting and unfortunate employee. The assumption is that many incidences of employee abuses originate from managers who have no interpersonal skills.

No one needs an empirical investigation to understand that employee emotional "abuse rarely manifests itself in an isolated incident, there is usually a pattern of abusive behaviour toward subordinates" (Bassman, 1992, p.5). Those abusive behaviours only make the employees powerless to defend themselves against the tyranny of cruel despotic managers and supervisors.

Danielle worked for over four years at a particular institution with a supervisor who was extremely unkind. During that time the supervisor relentlessly, and on a continuous basis sought to demean the employee in the presence of colleagues. At times, she made Danielle out to be incompetent, difficult to work with, and foolish. When the employee attempted to defend the unfairness, the supervisor usually ends up winning with "I will note this on your next review."

Any supervisor, who systematically intimidates and devalues an employee through words or actions, is exerting a noxious type of influence that will distill emotions of anger, fearfulness, passive aggression, or feelings of low self-esteem in the individual. Nevertheless, the abuse of employees is not a new[ii] situation that has recently evolved. Employee abuse has been active for a long time, but has become institutionalized in educational institutions and in corporate industries.

Institutional Abuse

"Institutional abuse" is another form many employees face on a daily basis. This is evidenced in areas such as "corporate culture, policies, procedures, and management practices that provide an environment supporting abuse" (Bassman, 1992, p. xiii). The question is "What recourse does an employee has in some of those situations?" While there may be in-house mechanisms for reporting violations, those persons who have to deal with the problems, are employees of the same employer. In most cases, it can be a catch twenty-two dilemma.

Besides, how many ombudspersons or Human Resource intervener would jeopardize a position to be honest and frank with another employee who is *just* another person and means nothing to him or her? Institutional abuse can lead to distress even more so when an employee does not have adequate representation for recourse.

Moreover, emotions drive us to do what we do (Goldie, 2002). Hence, the employee who is under pressure from unfair treatment might react and behave irrationally in an effort to be relieved from stress, and emotional strain. The assumption is that the suppression of emotions is not the ideal neither is irrational behaviour the answer for employee abuse. It is therefore in the interest of the individual to learn skills in the management of emotions to maintain a healthy work life and emotional balance both for the self and others.

Some Forms of Institutional Abuses
- Inequalities in vacation and sick time
- Discrimination of age, and gender
- Lack of or unfairness in promotional opportunities
- Lack of recognition of outstanding performance
- Stereotyping because of differences
- Racial discrimination
- Lack of recognition of educational abilities and specialized skills
- Cultural and social prejudices
- Overworking of employees with no compensation
- Use of veiled threats for compliance in order to increase productivity
- Control of employees' feelings
- Lack of personal development and self-improvement opportunities
- Confusion of roles and too many superiors
- Incompetent and untrained supervisors in interpersonal and conflict management skills
- Lack of confidentiality
- Unfair and unclear policies
- Injustices of all kinds directed to certain groups

Chapter 5   Workplace Stress

Workers face all kinds of challenges on a daily basis. Those events may require strenuous emotional efforts to make the right decisions. Furthermore, each day has its own complement of work-related events which can result in positive/negative, pleasant/unpleasant outcomes. Those outcomes might be the cause for emotional abuses from managers making the day more complicated. Moreover, if the outcome is negative and unpleasant, this will cause emotional strain, which will further inject toxins of resentment and hostilities in the environment.

Undeniably, each day there are many workplace situations, which influence the lives of employees with varying degrees of intensity. Those experiences often impinge on individual personalities, beliefs, culture, and personal differences, which may cause unhappiness and pain. Sometimes an employee seeks help for a violation, but is ignored or disappointed with the response from administrators. Everyone has personal and social needs for comfort, respect, appreciation, recognition, relationships, and esteem.

In the workplace, some needs are similar and basic to all employees. They include personal growth and development, promotion, self-actualization, opportunity to use judgment and problem-solve, inclusion, among others. The lack of fulfillment of those needs will leave a void in the life of the individual, and this causes stress.

Stress occurs when there are uncertainties, such as the future of one's job, lack of promotional opportunities, lack of yearly increment and bonuses, and so on. However, stress can be situational, and "refers to our reaction to a situation that poses demands, constraints, or opportunities usually not wanted" (Sarason & Sarason, 1996, p.5).

The response to stress is not the same for each individual because not everyone has the same coping skills for dealing with life-changing events. While one individual will be proactive in finding other alternatives, another person might consider a minor infraction to be magnanimous depending on the factors such as the weather, personal needs, and moods. The difference in response could be the way each person evaluates incidents, and the impact of the situation on the individual.[iii]

Everyone is vulnerable to stressful situations because of the daily interactions with people. There are differences of opinions, personalities, likes and dislikes, worldviews, needs, aspirations, and so on. In some employments, there are times when there are deadlines, short staff situations, threats of layoffs, and various other situations to create stress on an employee.

Other situations could be over-work, being under-paid, and underemployment. Those situations can be stressful especially if the individual is holding on to the job because of national economic climate and the difficulty in finding another position.

There are conditions, which will be stressful if employees work with people who are negative, pompous, hateful, racists, prejudiced, and outwardly obnoxious. Similar to many other workplace situations, the employee is not immune to stress regardless of the cause.

Furthermore, circumstances in the employee's life maybe contributors of stressful situations, which will add to the daily workplace challenges. A combination of the two conditions will create pressure, which might affect the employee's performance. Unless the employee learns how to cope with the pressing demands, emotions will dictate actions and behaviours.

Additionally, the suppression of emotions will cause stress if the individual works in an emotional overwhelming environment. Elements in such an environment might be racism, verbal insults, ostracism, and many unkind situations with no effective solutions.

If the individual does not learn how to manage emerging emotions, the impact leads to frustration, anxiety, and stress. There are times when an employee meets the qualifications for a certain position, but faces rejection for no apparent reasons.

In some cases when the refusal becomes repetitious, this can affect the emotional health of that individual. It is situations like those, which result in workplace stress. Still, it is in the employee's best interest to identify stressors and deal with them.

Chapter 6   Sources of Work Related Stress

There are many stress related situations in a given working environment, which will affect the employees. For example, the very thought of losing one's job will cause stress. Moreover, if there is rumour of lay-offs, this will make people become concerned for their jobs wondering who might be the victim/s. Another situation could be the employee who has to do multi-task activities with frequent interruptions. Most certainly, the interruptions alone can make the person irritable and angry. It is hard to predict what will happen or how each individual will react to stressful situations. One might take time off from work, while another complains or use sick days to escape stressful situations.

Work related stress also results from the defensive way people "react to situations in which they feel threatened and under pressure" (Bramson, 1981, pp.197-199). The reaction might not be physical, yet it creates deep psychological wounds affecting motivation and self-worth (p.199). For example, if a supervisor humiliates an employee in the presence of a colleague, the hurt person may not react openly, but might take a passive aggressive action to soothe the embarrassment. Feelings of intimidation, bullying, and threats will make an employee cower even when he or she should speak up against emotional crimes. Furthermore, when a supervisor stands over an employee while working, this alone will result in stress and nervousness. *Sylvia* had such an experience.

> *"My supervisor would stand behind me while I work, not because I could not do the work or was lazy. Her aim was to intimidate and control me by any means possible. I would be shaking and sweating while she stood behind me. It was awful."*

Another way in which the injured employee may react is not to take part in office parties unless it is unavoidable. People will use several ways of coping with workplace stress by their reactions to the emotional impact of an incident.[iv] This is so true even if it means damaging equipment, or delaying work.

There are many sources of work-related stress such as environmental, organizational, and individual conditions[v]. Including are intimidation, unfairness, lack of promotion, emotional strain, and racial injustices. Any or a combination of those factors among other things can affect an employee causing stress. Since each person is unique with different personalities, coping skills, and temperaments, stress will affect each individual in a different way.

Environmental Stress Factors

These factors could include conditions such as fear and receiving unfair treatment from a supervisor. One worker recalls having butterflies each time the supervisor approaches because she was always so critical and threatening. According to the employee, the supervisor was kind and gentle to others, but reversed the behaviour towards her. Another reason could also be harassment or the supervisor recording every infraction no matter how slight. These are situations, which will put the employee in bondage because he or she has to walk on eggshells when in the presence of an unscrupulous supervisor.

A particular case is the situation where a supervisor gave a project to two employees. Within a day, when one of the worker was out, on her return she discovered the supervisor had changed her mind, and gave all the work to one person while the other worker flew around like a butterfly. After making enquiries concerning the sudden change, the supervisor's response was, "I want *you* to do all the work." The worker was extremely disappointed, and went on to do the job. However, she took her time and completed the task longer than the arranged schedule. This was a case of open racial prejudice in the particular situation. Both were of different ethnicities. You be the judge of who was what.

Organizational Stress Factors

The organizational source relates to organizational structure, the demands made on employees, stringent rules, fear of lay-offs, and unfavourable policies. In terms of demands, in some situations the expectation is for the employee to work long hours with no extra time off or monetary compensation.

In addition, some employees are often required to take vacations at certain times and not when they desire. Naturally, there are times when according to the nature of work certain departments must have a full complement of staff to meet needs. For example, an employee who works as an accountant will be required to be present the month or weeks preceding the end of a fiscal year. Furthermore, those who work in educational institutions must be present at certain times when students need financial help. Nevertheless, there are other situations where policies are suddenly changed, and employees have to accept or seek for alternative employment.

In some cases, employees face the threat of termination daily only because a supervisor hates the individual. That person seeks for any opportunity to reprimand even if there are no apparent reasons only to hasten the time of departure. Often those types of supervisors act on a sudden impulse to change the employee's status with some frivolous reasons. These are organizational situations, which will cause or contribute to stress in the workplace.

In one case, an individual worked in an institution for over ten years and left there emotionally broken, disillusioned, frustrated, and depressed. The departure came suddenly after years of emotional stress, humiliation, verbal assaults, racial discrimination, and frustration received from a vindictive supervisor.

Stacy. When I worked in such an atmosphere, I told myself that after I had accomplished certain goals I would leave for a better position somewhere else. However, time caught up on me unawares, and leaving would mean starting all over again in another place. Evidently, the only alternative was to remain in the position until retirement. Although this was a reasonable decision, it was difficult because the abuse became extremely unbearable with regular visits to the doctor until he became tired of the frequent visits to his office. In fact, a threatening situation occurred, which made me escape for my life. Remaining in that position was at the expense of my emotional health. My working experience at that office was in every way unhealthy because of the pressures I had to endure from incompetent supervisors who lacked interpersonal and managerial skills.

Referring to organizational stress, listen to the story of Moira who worked in a higher education institution.

I worked with Fred for many years. During this time, he showed respect, in his way, and pretended that I was part of the group. However, I noticed that whenever visitors came to the department, he would pass by my desk and take the person to others, and introduce the visitor to them. After a while, I thought, "What is going on here?" He passed by me, went over and made the introductions, but said nothing to me. I mentioned my observation to someone and made the comment that "I must be a ghost."

Individual Stress Factors

Research reported that, "the nature of stress can be psychological, and this depends on where the individual has the strongest commitment because they are personal and important" (Lazarus & Lazarus, 1994, p.229). This is quite true. Commitment can relate to the need to maintain a stable working experience. It could also mean situations requiring the person to remain in that position until retirement, to provide for the family or to complete a course of study. If the employee is concerned about financial insecurities, this will affect the performance and the emotional stability.

According to Robbins (1991), economic problems created by individuals when they over-extend their financial resources would cause stress and distract them from their work. Still, while an individual's problems can create stressors; other problems exist in the workplace, which will affect that person.

Individual stress, whatever the source, causes various physiological and psychological symptoms expressed in the workplace. Therefore, if the working environment is emotionally unhealthy, a combination of negative situations, only compound the stress factor; and this will certainly affect the individual's health and behaviour. Those physiological symptoms include headaches, increased blood pressure, and induced heart attacks (Robbins 1991, p.614).

From the psychological perspective, the symptoms include tension, and anxiety. Stress may change the behaviour of the individual will resulting in substance abuse, smoking, anger, frequent absences, and changes in eating habits. Obviously, not only the employee may be in this situation, but also the temperamental supervisor who will administer verbal and emotional abuses to an unsuspecting employee.

Unfairness and Lack of Promotion

The unfair denial of promotion, and undue pressure to train a new employee for a position in which the present employee is active will create stress. It is unfair to ask someone to train another for the very position the employee held for years without justifiable reasons for denial of promotion.

In one situation, after receiving an excellent review, the employee was denied the position, yet was asked to train the new employee.

What is most disturbing in another situation is when a supervisor told a worker her overall performance was below the required expectation. The supervisor gave the employee two weeks' notice to quit, while in the same breath asked to train a new worker for the same job. The worker refused to teach the new employee.

Fairly speaking, if the performance of the individual was not satisfactory to the supervisor, how then could this person train the new employee for the same job?

One might ask if such a situation does happen in the workplace. The answer is that it does happen. Situations like those are conditions, which cause dissatisfaction and create stress in the life of individuals.

Emotional Strain and Poor Health

While research has reported that stress is one of the major maladies of recent times, the workplace seems to be an arable ground for this condition to grow and develop. When the presence of stress becomes part of the daily intake of the employee's tasks this results in "poor psychological or physical health or cause risk factors making poor health more likely" (Beehr, 1995, p.11).

Poor emotional health associated with the workplace environment can be the result of the strains experienced by the worker, which are harmful to the physical and personal well-being of that individual.

Argumentatively, the strain from stress does not necessarily have to be the result from daily tasks, but it could likely be from the constant display of emotions the employee does not feel, but have to exhibit in order to adhere to stringent policies. Beehr further noted that the strains "are the outcome of stress and they correspond to poor health" (p.109).

Those who suffer emotional strain include workers in educational institutions who have to deal with unruly, disrespectful, and undisciplined students who believe they have a right to behave however way they choose because they are paying for their tuition.

There are also donors to those institutions who are openly mean and abusive to workers, especially those at the front desk whom some will treat with disdain. What is most appalling about those situations is that senior administrators, deans, and professors ignore students and donors abusive behaviours.

Therefore, the emotionally assaulted worker has to take whatever treatment which comes with the job. Those persons have to remain calm and detached with an impersonal demeanour and an attitude of "it's all in a day's work" in order to hold on to the job

Racial Injustices

Racism *is* a factor of workplace stress. It is complex because it blends easily in each of the situations noted. Anyone who has ever experienced this demon knows the emotional pain it brings with its sisters prejudice, discrimination, and bigotry. This evil demonstrates itself in unfairness, biases, injustices, and partiality. Racism is a wicked and dangerous behaviour humanity has ever known.

Racism can only survive in an organizational environment through the behaviour of individuals who are usually in management position, at whatever level that might be. Most of the stories in this text have elements of this monster, which the employees experienced during their working life in higher educational institutions.

Mara stated that at an interview the interviewer made a sarcastic remark the nature of which was not required for either the interview or the position. She responded, but of course did not receive the job.

Racism is usually a common cause for lack of promotion in an institution. With a situation such as racism, while there are laws and organizational policies to curb its activities, it still exists. None of the agents of change will be able to eradicate it completely, so long as there are people who do not care for the welfare and feelings of other human beings.

Work-related stress has no discrimination or respect of persons. It will affect anyone in the workplace. If management and administrators in organizations discover any of those sources of work-related stresses, they should make every effort to eliminate or reduce those stressors.

Support should come from all areas of management, and employees must report situations, which are emotionally hurtful to them.

In any case, an organization can do nothing unless the employee makes reports concerning any form of emotional abuse. Whether there is recourse or positive response, the fact that a report is made and documented will be in the best interest of the employee if the conditions worsened.

Nevertheless, since people have situations in their lives to cause stress, no workplace can do everything to rid any individual of stress. Stress is a part of the working world.

Chapter 7 **Employees Fears**

There are employees present and past, who will bear witness of being under constant fear in the workplace. Those fears are real, and not a made-up pretend emotion. The reality is that the working environment of this millennium is becoming physically and emotionally destructive. There was a time when maybe one could speak only of emotional pain; but of recent times, there have been many incidences reported of physical hurt whilst on the job.

Although an individual seems calm and unmoved after an abuse does not mean there is no feeling of pain. That pain is often internal and only the individual knows how he or she feels. Fear will make an employee withdrawn and internalize feelings from humiliating and disgusting events. Usually, the origin of workplace fear comes from an insensitive despotic supervisor who does not demonstrate professional ethics. Those persons abuse their authority by directing their power in ways to bring about constant fear in the lives of those whom they manage. When people work under severe strain, they will react after constantly absorbing emotional abuses. They become like a soggy sponge dripping with emotional pain. In a working environment where fear is evident, an employee may choose to dull the emergent feelings until there is a safe convenient place to express it.

Reaction to unfair treatment may not occur immediately, but this does not mean the individual does not experience some form of emotional sensation. Very often, employees who suffer emotional abuse in the form of fear do not react covertly mainly because of what the consequences might be. Therefore, they hide their feelings because no one will believe such things. What is even worse is that in some institutions and corporate places, those in senior positions are on pedestals as "untouchables."

Obviously, dare *anyone* bring an accusation against his or her behaviours and performance? Who will believe any adverse reports from an aggrieved employee about those tyrants? Evidently, the employee who works for one of those oppressors is in a difficult situation because he or she is not important. The unfortunate employee may cover feelings of hurt. Others spend more time at the doctors for symptoms for which there are no evident causes. Furthermore, doctors' time is such an expensive commodity these days, they may not spend time to delve into the causes for symptoms in order to make referrals.

Consequently, the emotionally abused employee's only help is to identify and name those feelings with precise descriptive language to bring out their intensity. Moreover, the doctor cannot use his stethoscope to identify invisible emotional pain. It is the responsibility of the employee to report feelings, to obtain the right kind of help. The fact that emotion abuse is not easily identifiable as one would another condition, makes it even harder for someone to understand the sufferer or to believe him or her. Unfortunately, that person endures internal anguish and pain over long periods with no professional help. *Marla's* situation became unbearable after working with her manager for many years. According to her,

> *Despite complaints to senior personnel, no one paid any attention. Although there were several visits to the doctor, he only prescribed medication to make me sleep at nights. However, after a while the doctor's behaviour showed that he was tired of seeing me in his office because of my frequent visits. On a particular day, I called to make an appointment and the secretary said to me, "that depends on whether Dr.... wants to see you." Well, that made me recoil and I did not go back to see him, until I was forced to do because he was my primary care physician. Even when I went, I noticed the secretary would treat me as if I were an intruder. What they did not understand is that I was working under severe pressures. It is true that I should have left, but there were many reasons why I continued working, and for those reasons, I waited until it was time for me to leave, or rather, I ran for my life when I was assaulted by the same supervisor.*

Since we want others to think well of us, there is the temptation to let a supervisor's inappropriate behaviour go unnoticed without making mention about incidences of abuse. Furthermore, the fear of losing one's job is a major factor for keeping quiet about workplace abuses. Seemingly, some managers, and supervisors believe it is there given right to treat an employee with unacceptable behaviours. Those behaviours often lead to interpersonal conflicts. What those persons fail to understand is that, "supervisors are charged with the responsibility of managing others..." and they "should be skilled at initiating direct talk to solve problems with co-workers..." (Slaikeu & Hasson, 1998 p.114).

Unfortunately, this appears to be quite the opposite in many cases especially when an employee is from a background considered minority or where there is language, cultural, gender, economic, and educational differences. Notwithstanding, while the abused employee may not verbalize feelings, the body language and behaviours might communicate to the supervisor he is not satisfied with the treatment demonstrated.

For example, even if there is fear, that person will show hurt by his behaviour after unfair treatment. In fact, some employees received threats of losing their jobs, demotion, or with an unfair performance review. Many supervisors and managers abuse their powers and treat employees with scant respect; yet they expect to receive respect and regard from the employees.

Since emotional awareness is the way we experience an emotional feeling, what we do with the feeling requires careful thought. Additionally, internal biological stimuli stimulate our emotions after an encounter with an event. Sometimes the employee may not respond to those feelings immediately. Later there is the tendency to recall past experiences, and it is from those memories that response to an emotion occurs if the event repeats itself (*See Schachter & Singer, 2001*).

Past occurrences of events become deciding factors to guide the individual how to respond to similar events. Although the situations and persons may be different, yet the fact that something similar happened before will make the person want to plan a way for managing a new event.

Fear of the consequences of expressing emotions will make the employee choose to put up with maltreatment and insults, rather than seek for recourse. In another situation where fear is present, the individual must decide whether to flee or argue with a manager who has been insulting and disrespectful. Fear may be for physical harm or from anger, which might be destructive. It may sound unusual, but there have been occasions when an employee feels threatened by the behaviour of a manager, or even other employees.

Another reason for fear could be that a confrontation might create a hostile environment, so the offended person may delay a response after a put down from a manager until when face-to-face in his office. An employee might not want to admit to fear of another employee or manager because this might seem foolish.

Nevertheless, when there are reasons for fear, they should be dealt with immediately to prevent other serious psychological problems for the individual. Fear brings torment therefore, it would be impossible for the individual to remain in a balanced state of mind.

Another reason for the prevalence of fear in the workplace is the suppression of an employee's intellectual abilities. For instance, when an employee is told "you should *only* seek positions at the support level" even though that person has leadership skills, and possesses graduate level degrees, this is demeaning. Those situations are not mere fantasies; rather, they are real employee experiences. Why should an employee be fearful in such a situation? There are many reasons.

For example, if a would-be future employer obtains information from the immediate supervisor/manager, the former has the employee's future in his hand. There seems to be an internal network, which often works to keep some employees from promotions. Usually, one can trace the reasons to the immediate employer who feels threatened for whatever reasons.

Clearly, the awareness of an emotion such as fear will influence the employee's thought pattern. Frequently, people react from their imaginations and perceptions. Those thoughts could be false and may create problems both for themselves and for others. The person who has a positive and active thought pattern will analyze and process information with questions of "why," "what," "when," "who," and "how" before making conclusive decisions about the reason for a given situation.

It is true that we should not ignore our emotions because they are natural to our being. Emotions are necessary for change, and for solving problems to enhance interpersonal relationships. However, it is important for both employer and employees to be aware of those emotions, which result in conflict situations.

According to Marsha, she literally cried every morning before she went to work because the environment was so hostile and unbearable. She said that she suffered from insomnia and various types of psychosomatic problems. This is how she described her immediate boss.

Bob is very efficient, but treats the workers as inanimate objects, and no different from the furniture and equipment. He is a micro manager and blows things out of proportion. Everyone is afraid and has to walk as if on eggshells. He rules with an iron rod, and his handshake is similar to holding a hedgehog. The environment is intimidating, stiff as steel and hard as flint. Hardly does anyone smiles or seems pleasant.

Clearly, in such an environment workers live in emotional bondage if they are unable to express themselves. The examples given corroborate the writers' arguments that emotions are associated with feelings and experiences, physiology and behaviour, and cognitions and conceptualizations (Ortony, Clore, & Collins, 1988, p.1). The expression of feelings is with facial expressions, language, and communication. Consequently, in a working environment where social interaction is limited, the impact of this arrangement will create behaviours of interpersonal and emotional conflicts.

Some Reasons for Employees Concerns

- Wrongful accusations
- Lack of respect from immediate employers
- Being treated as an inferior
- Ethnic, language, educational, economic, gender, personal values, and social differences
- Deceptive employers

- Physical attacks
- Ostracism
- Being ridiculed for various reasons
- Being ignored
- Being laid off
- Not being promoted or given a raise
- Various types of unfair treatment
- Fear of a poor performance review

Chapter 8 Masking of Feelings

Occasionally, we mask our feelings because of where we are, the person who is present, or if only to ignore an obnoxious person with whom we do not wish to enter into conversation. We make this voluntary choice for our own benefit and not as an expectation or under coercion. For example, if we are working with someone who is unkind, loud, and rude we will try to avoid interacting with that person. We do everything in our power not to speak or smile because we consider the individual objectionable. Therefore, even though we might want to laugh at a joke we restrain ourselves. We set our faces to communicate disgust, shock, rebuff, and other signals to tell the person we do not wish to interact. Nevertheless, masking our feelings or pretending an event did not occur, will not change the emergent emotion after the event. Pretense only acts as a momentary band-aid to cover up, while intra-psychic processes are at work in response to the emotions an individual is experiencing.

Emotions are communication stimuli used to inform others about our feelings. They also act as feedback devices when someone responds to a stimulus whether negative or positive. Although some emotions are controllable, some are not so easy to manage. For instance, we automatically become fearful at the sight of danger. Despite those situations, employees who work in an emotionally oppressive environment will find that there are times when they will have to mask their emotions for the benefit of being a good team player, to maintain the status quo, and to promote good-will for the institution or corporation. Those employees work under pressure because the emotions are stifled in order to comply with the rules and policies of their employers.

Normally people hide behind their feelings as a choice and not as a prescriptive expectation in order to please someone or an establishment. The masking of feelings means the employee must not reveal hurt or show embarrassment when a customer or even a superior behaves inappropriately. There are educational institutions where agents will reprimand a worker for responding to a rude student. In one situation, a student shouted at a worker and openly demeaned the individual. The dean, who overheard the altercation from the beginning and knew that the student was out of place, took the student to her office and soothed her, but later severely castigated the worker in the most embarrassing and distressful manner.

The worker returned shaking because the student was the one at fault, but received justice. Should we react to abuse immediately as it happens? Should we ignore emotional abuses? Why should we even mask our feelings? In any case, whether there is just cause or not, it is not always easy to mask the way we feel. The reason is that, although we might not verbalize the way we feel, our expressions of surprise, and disapproval are signs of discomfort, or displeasure about an event.

Furthermore, if an employee allows abuse to go on indefinitely, over time the effect will eventually affect the person's health both emotionally and physically. The individual may become irritable, stressful, frustrated, and sometimes difficult to work with. Moreover, the situation may worsen, and treatment might be necessary because the suppression of the emotions impinge on other areas of the body resulting in increased symptoms.

> In some cases where the emotional tension is prolonged, palpitation of the heart may occur so readily that the person suffering from it may no longer be aware of the emotional stress that originally triggered it. He then becomes filled with new fears…Sometimes a person's emotional conflicts are so difficult for him to accept that he represses his feelings…and is no longer consciously aware of them (Narramore, 1960, p.163).

Some Reasons for Masking
Personal Values
Masking of feelings could be the result of the employee's personal values and beliefs. Those principles may be cultural or religious. The values become principles by which he conducts his behaviours and they will be the deciding factors when dealing with emotional situations. For that individual the masking of emotions become second nature.

Employer Requirements
Another reason could be an immediate employer's selfish requirements programmed into the individual's psyche. Those requirements could be the misinterpretation of policies, which make the daily routine of the employee arduous.

To avoid Confrontation
There are people who mask their feelings to avoid confrontation because of the way they view themselves. If they do not accept their limitations, personality traits, or if they lack self-acceptance, those persons will not want to face difficulties. Obviously, they will avoid any kinds of provocations if this means opening themselves to criticisms. Acceptance comes from the inside out and brings about satisfaction and fulfillment (Hibbert, 2002, p.6).

Fear of Intimidation
Another reason why an employee would mask feelings is the fear of intimidation from supervisor or manager. Intimidation will become a force built by an abuser against another who seems somewhat weaker. Employees who feel intimidation from a *bully* supervisor is working in a psychologically abusive atmosphere. Psychological abuse is hard to identify and for this reason, many employees suffer at the hands of cruel supervisors and managers. Really, masking emotions is only a camouflage to cover the way an individual feels about any harmful event.

Fear of receiving Unfair Appraisal

Another example could be an employee who is fearful of receiving an unfair performance appraisal from a supervisor. When the appraisal seems unfair, the employee will be disappointed and might respond with behaviours of anger, resentment or he might repress the feelings. Repression might be in the form of masking the emotion of disappointment. The masking of emotions is "especially emphasized in accounts of middle management and most professions (Wharton & Erickson, 1993, p.467).

Nonetheless, the employee who represses his emotions believes that self-control is better than expressing one's feelings. In such a situation, delay in addressing problems might only prolong and institutionalize unfair practices. In addition, repressing one's feelings only temporarily numb for a while, but on a continuous basis, the individual will eventually lose the awareness of his emotions. In fact, he loses the sharpness of certain emotions that could alert him when to approach an individual and when to withdraw. The constant abuse of one's emotions will eventually kill the sensory feelings that would protect him from further abuse.

Notwithstanding, another individual may not want to mask his feelings and prefers to express them to show contempt for maltreatment and unfairness from insensitive employers' agents. The inference is that emotions are "motivators for the behaviour meant to deal with an emotional event" (Lazarus & Lazarus, 1994, p.114). While this is true, there are times when masking is the ideal route to take because of where the event took place. Unquestionably, if an aggrieved employee becomes expressively emotional because he believes he has been unfairly assessed by a supervisor his "perceived impropriety of the act, then, is likely to stimulate the experience of anger and resentment" (Johnson, Ford, & Kaufman, 2000, p.117).

Reviewing an hypothetical situation

1.   *Make sure the complaint is abuse*
2.   *Are you initiating this abuse because of your*
     - Performance
     - Lateness
     - Lack of team spirit
     - Being anti-social
     - Difficult to work with
     - Frequent absences without explanations

3.   *If you are clear with the items in [2] then*
- Name the abuser
- Identify and name the abuse using clear descriptive language
- Produce dates, place, antecedents, times, and any witnesses
- Do not leave personal information on your computer
- Do not use company email for personal business
- Report your feelings to the abuser
- Attend to your health, changes in your mood, sleep, and eating habits, etc.
- Check with the company/institution policy manual about abuse, discrimination, and harassment
- You may need to go and see your doctor who *might* refer you to a psychologist
- Find out about internal resources for making complaints, e.g., mediator, ombudsperson, or human resource
- Keep a record of all incidences with your responses and compare with company policies

4.   *If you have done all you can and everything failed, it is time to seek outside help*
- Government agencies to address your type of situation
- Legal advice
- Do not aggravate the situation with threats or unsociable behaviours.

When an individual masks true feelings it might be that he does not have the courage to confront an aggressor. We have heard the saying that a person's bark is more hurtful than his bite. Nevertheless, a loud harsh bark can be just as hurtful as a bite. Some supervisors build impenetrable walls making employees fearful of confrontation about situations that cause hurt and pain. Clearly, if employees who suffer abuse would monitor and dialogue those situations and speak up at an appropriate time, there is the probability that the behaviour might change.

Still, employees will attest that even after bringing the situation to the instigator with no change, taking it further could well be just as useless. In those situations, the next step should be finding some type of outside recourse that will intervene in order to resolve the problem, or finding a new position.

All employees should know that being quiet and passive, makes them targets for abuses from managers who are juvenile in their behaviours. Even if the abusers are professors, deans, and CEOs, with the highest educational credentials, the employee should make reports of their behaviours or at least keep documentation of all occurrences. The employees themselves can become their worst enemy when they do not address abuses affecting their health and peace of mind. Masking emotions will not always help, but can become very painful to the one who do not seek help.

Chapter 9   Suppression of Emotions

Emotional suppression is an inherent factor in the life of every individual because there are times when it is not appropriate to express oneself in a manner that would prove destructive. However, in a workplace setting where people spend many hours on a daily basis, if hurtful feelings are constantly suppressed, after a while this can prove dangerous to an employee.

To suppress here would mean employing internal pressure to control an emergent emotion in an attempt to prevent or de-escalate conflict. It could also mean that the individual is holding back to please institutional requirements. Understandably, emotions have both negative and positive responses depending on the type of event evoking them. Nevertheless, the expression of emotions must be in a controlled manner.

Ledoux 1994, argued that "in the presence of an emotional stimulus, the brain evaluates the significance of that stimulus and on the basis of that evaluation produces responses appropriate to the meaning of the stimulus" (p.270).

If this is so, one can only assume that emotional suppression must place a considerable amount of strain on the individual who has to respond according to the dictates of employer regulations. It means that the individual must always be on guard for the evaluation of negative events in order to emit the expected response at any given moment.

The question is "What effect does this behaviour have on the employee over a period of time?" "How does this constant alertness coupled with performance affect the individual's life?" Ledoux's findings showed that "to be effective, voluntary responses must be based on information about the stimulus, the situation, and possible outcomes of actions" (p.272).

In contrast, "involuntary, hard-wired responses eliminate the need for decision" (p.272). Therefore, the employee who has to model his behaviour would draw upon learned behaviours or prescriptions laid out by his employers that will eventually become automatic.

Eventually, the result from an emotional abuse will be a ready smile in the face of rebuke from customers, students, or clients because of the learned behaviour, which has become routine. The employee will respond almost unconsciously with a performance suitable for any occasion.

Contrastingly, the employee who does not care for his job security or prescriptive employer expectations will certainly "eliminate the need for decision" and act according to how he feels about an abusive event.

The suppression of emotions is different from masking. While masking is an act of pretense by using a false front to please, with suppression the employee restrains feelings and demonstrates acceptable behaviours for the benefit of the employer. Both situations can later prove injurious to the individual's health.

In a series of studies carried out by (Levenson, 1994, pp.273-279) "regarding the effects of suppression" he discovered that the "visible signs of emotion involves real work, and that this work makes significant metabolic demands" (p.278).

Furthermore, Levenson's argued that, "emotions call forth powerful motor programs that mobilize activity in the muscles of the face, trunk, the limbs, and other parts of the body" collaborates with other findings mentioned earlier.

In addition, he reported that, "these motor programs enable the organism to adapt rapidly to the environmental demands that provoked the emotion" (p.278).

Clearly then, at any given moment, the employee must quickly adjust feelings in response to the emotional prescription of an institution regardless of how painful an event might be.

This is when suppression can prove dangerous to the health of the individual. This point is borne out most significantly in Levenson's report, which stated that, "findings suggesting that certain kinds of emotional inhibition may well have adverse health consequences" (p.279).

It is unimaginable to assume that the daily pressures of having to pretend against one's natural biological feelings will not affect the health, and cause emotional and physical problems. This is similar to going against traffic where someone's negligence results in the injury or death of another.

There are workplaces requiring the suppression of emotional exhibitions to display "the customer is always right" maxim in order to keep the job or to look good in the eyes of the beholder no matter how uncomfortable a situation might be (see Hochschild, 1983).

Working under those conditions requires the employee to be *consistently, carefully,* and *intentionally* monitor and manage emotions with the understanding that *only* the *correct* ones will be effective and acceptable in a given situation.

In view of the current national economic situation, it would not be surprising that there are workers who will remain in certain positions rather than face indefinite unemployment. When a job seeker reads a description requiring total submission to all types of employer/client/customer abuses, this is an example of the subtleness of this insidious occupational crime against the worker.

Hochschild (1983) affirmed that, "even when people are paid to be nice, it is hard for them to be nice at all times and when their efforts succeed, it is a remarkable accomplishment" (p.118).

Unmistakably, the suppression of emotions is detrimental to one's health, because this type of emotional pretense is a "display of emotional neutrality and restraint" (Wharton & Erickson, 1993, p.464).

The presumption is that there are "rules" (Hochschild, 1983 p.89), some implicit and others explicit, in the place of employment where workers are expected to behave according to management behavioural specifications, whether that behaviour is harmful to the person's mental health, personal beliefs, or values.

Obviously, "roles requiring high degrees of emotion management are those where role performance demands constant attentiveness to emotional display" (Wharton & Erickson, 1993, p.463).

However, when an employee obeys an organization's emotional prescription and accepts abuses from a [*valued*] customer, who advocates for that individual? Who cares about the employee's feelings or health? Will the employee be commended for being "obedient" in pleasing the employer? Take for instance the case of *Tandie*:

> *I had worked for six years with my supervisor. On a particular day, I received a call from a male whose voice I did not recognize, and who asked to speak to the Executive Officer [title change]. I asked for his name and his response was "I will not give you my name. Just give me..." I insisted, but he was adamant and very rude. When the EO came, I told him about the conversation. Later, I overheard him talking with the same man: "oh, that was only the assistant." I felt mortified because his nonchalant manner made me feel as if I were an item in the office, an object for abuse. I had no recourse but to return to my desk. It turned out that the individual had to be pleasantly accommodated because he was making a large donation to the... That was the end of the matter.*

Presumably, the employee alluded to above had to accept the abuse from the donor because he is valued and his contribution is more important than the feelings of an employee. Even so, I believe the EO could have softened the blow somewhat, but he did not.

When an individual suppresses painful emotions from hurtful events, the result might lead to passive aggressive behaviours, decrease in productivity, animosities, hostilities, disrespect, and poor interpersonal relationships.

The suppression of emotions will only solve problems for a short time, but cannot serve as a long-term healthy response for the individual who faces problems in the workplace.

Notwithstanding, the emotional life of the individual is very important because it can promote either good health or illness (Lazarus & Lazarus, 1994, p.39).

Therefore, no one should have to suppress pain on a daily basis only to remain employed. There may not be an alternative, but to leave the place of employment in order to keep one's sanity and dignity.

What Employers Can Do

Since corporations and institutions are only entities, the owners and management boards have to employ others to get the work done. However, while applicants may possess superb academic and technical qualifications, many lack the necessary managerial skills for effective communication and interpersonal relationships. Frequently, employees blame the place of employment and use negative expressive terms against it.

Admittedly, many times the policies are often unfriendly in some places, yet the managers they hire usually create unpleasant experiences for unsuspecting employees. Institutions and corporations can help to ease many of the problems caused by problematic managers and supervisors who are untrained in interpersonal and conflict management skills.

1. Each manager/supervisor should be on probation similar to the regular employees.

2. There should be employee performance review about immediate employers such as managers and supervisors, who report on other employees.

3. When a manager repeatedly gives a negative report on an employee, this should be investigated because there must be some weaknesses either in his managerial expertise or the employee needs help.

Chapter 10   Emotions

Emotions are natural feelings, which influence our lives and behaviours every day. They are evident in the way we talk, the things we do, and the response we give to events. Emotions are also a type of universal language for communication. Our emotions can speak even when there is a language barrier. We yawn and immediately someone thinks that we are either hungry or sleepy. We knit our brows, shiver in the cold, smile, and others understand us without a word being spoken.

Emotions can be spontaneous, but are controllable for a number of personal, social, professional, or ethical reasons. Research shows that "ethicists have ignored emotions or thought them evaluatively unimportant…" holding that "emotions are abnormal…." The writer further stated that emotions are also "naturally thought of as misleading, disrupting, or even overwhelming" (Stocker, 2002, p.65). It is true that emotions can be misleading because tears do not always tell the true story of what the individual is feeling. For example, some individuals cry while they are watching a movie or because they are happy.

Furthermore, emotions can be disrupting because anger can cause work stoppage, animosities, fear, and alienation from others. Finally, when someone receives bad news, this can be overwhelming to the individual. Consequently, one could not accept that emotions are unimportant or abnormal; they are integral to our life in a variety of ways for communication and expression.

Another point is that emotions originate from the affective domain and can be expressed physiologically, or psychologically. One way of describing an emotion could be the response an individual expresses to an injury or pleasantness, whether verbal or physical. If someone feels hurt or shame from an event, those emotions are negative. However, when someone is pleased about an occasion that person will demonstrate this pleasure with smiles, giggles, or laughter. Emotions can also be placid, for example, when someone remains calm after a wrongful accusation. It can be harsh such as when anger becomes destructive.

Additionally, if someone received unfavourable news, the person might feel physical distress such as an increase in the heart rate or nervousness. Those are physiological stimulations resulting from the knowledge of the news and its effect on the individual. In another situation, an employee might receive a negative review from a supervisor that might result in anxiety and frustration, and eventually leads to stress.

There are many kinds of emotions including joy, happiness, contentment, and love. Others include rage, anger, hatred, aggression, verbal abuse, malice, resentment, and so on. These also include feelings evolving from our interpretation of past or present events in our lives. Depending on the outcome of cognitive evaluations, we then make our decisions as to how we will respond. The choice of response depends on whether the outcome of the evaluation is negative or positive according to the individual's perception of the event.

However, "emotions can arise without social or communicative stimuli," but, "even in those instances emotions are usually the result of imagined or anticipated interactions" (Andersen & Guerrero, 1998, p.58). In such a situation, the individual may have butterflies in the stomach at the thought of meeting someone for the first time, or being in the presence of a tyrant manager.

Communication Cues

Emotions are communication cues suggesting to the observer that an offense has been committed, or there is pleasure concerning an event. Additionally, an emotional signal will either make the observer approach or turn away.

Value

Stocker (2002) pointed out that "emotions are useful for revealing value" (p.69). Therefore, the impact of an encounter to an individual plays a significant role in the assignment of value to an event to facilitate an effective response. For instance, the person might judge the event as negligible, and ignore it as an accidental encounter, rather than something to harm or hurt. There is an indication here that *value* has a role in making the distinction as to what will be significant as opposed to what will not be important to an individual concerning an event. Evidently, emotions "provide evidence for our symptoms of value" (Planalp, 1999, p.165), making them important because they act as guides to help us understand events in order to make the right decisions.

Interest

Another important factor is that the emotive person must have some type of interest in the emotion for it to affect his feelings. This interest could be an indication to motivate the individual to either change an offensive behaviour or move to action.

Personal Life Drama

Another feature of emotion depicts it as "a personal life drama, which has to do with the fate of our goals in a particular encounter, our beliefs about ourselves and the world we live" (Lazarus & Lazarus, 1994, p.151). When an event takes place that affects our emotions, what causes us to react to those emotions? Can we point to the rush of adrenaline or is there some other explanation that motivates the individual to respond?

Lazarus & Lazarus (1994) alluded to two distinctive factors necessary to arouse an emotion. First, "an event must transform a routine encounter into one that involves personal harm or benefit." Second, "the way we judge the fate or outcome, determines whether the emotion will be positive or negative" (p.140). Since "an event must transform a routine encounter into one that involves personal harm or benefit," then an emotional encounter resulting in humiliation will make the individual feel some type of hurt to the self-esteem. Moreover, the employee who receives a notice of dismissal knows this will upset his routine – going out to work, his economic status, and his peace of mind. The assumption is that the effectiveness of an emotion depends on whether there is a particular goal at stake. Otherwise, an encounter with another person or the environment will not be emotional (p.140). The event will have no effect if the individual considers it as accidental, and not something detrimental.

Moral Emotions

Stocker, however, concedes that emotions such as shame, guilt, regret, remorse, all have something in common because they bear upon morality. In fact, the writer agrees that those are the "moral emotions" (p.148). Definitely, those moral emotions provide an individual with an approach or orientation to assist in the assessment of the attitude towards the self. Those emotions are principles by which many govern their lives.

When morals guide an individual, that person will analyze behaviours before allowing emotional outbursts to over rule a response. Therefore, an employee will mask or suppress emotions because of moral, cultural or religious principles. For instance, on the one hand shame acts as a constraint when the individual realize he has not lived up to a certain expectation by looking at what he has become. Shame can also be the response to an insult in the presence of others. Guilt on the other hand, is another set of injunctions alerting the individual that he has transgressed by what he has done (Wollheim, 1999, p.155).

The Complexity of Emotion

Emotions are complex reactions incorporating thoughts and behaviours, our minds and our body.[vi] This complexity of emotions explains the involvement of cognitive, psychological, and physiological structures. [*See Figure 2 below*]. Furthermore, the complexity of an emotion shows the interrelationship of those three areas, psychological – *emotions/feelings*, physiological – *body changes/behaviour*, and cognitive – *thinking/evaluation* showing their involvement when an event occurs. The three areas interact through the *affective* - emotions, *cognitive* - thinking processes, resulting in *behaviour* - actions, and *physiological* changes, e.g., goose bumps, racing heart. The interaction is an indication of the correlation of conflict and emotions resulting in psychological or physiological responses.

Apparently, when an event takes place we evaluate the emotion we feel and deal with it through our thinking process with internal conversations. Those conversations can be negative or positive. The outcome of the self-talk will assist in the decision for the type of response from the event.

When an incident occurs, the individual processes the event through thinking (cognitive), and feelings (affective) in an attempt to find meaning, and to make decisions whether to ignore, or pursue. The outcome of the exercise will bring about a response to the event through physiological, psychological, and behavioural expressions. The response might be proactive or reactive. Still, there are people who do not take time to process an incident and therefore, act impulsively.

Take for example a reprimand from a supervisor in the presence of others. The employee evaluates the event and the outcome could make her think the supervisor hates her or is being unfair. The emotions the incident might produce could be *anger, rejection, sadness, shame,* or *revenge*. The diagram below gives a picture of the complexity of emotions and the involvement of thinking, feelings, and active responses.

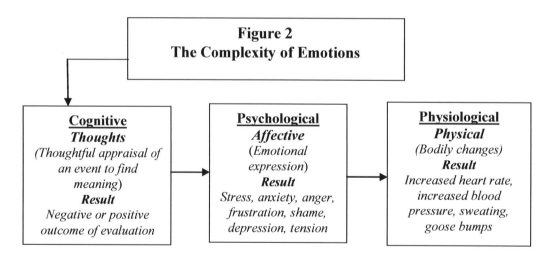

Copyright © Diagram adapted by B.Y. Stuart, 2013

Finally, emotions are feelings we use to express ourselves for others to understand us. Although in some workplaces employees are expected to act as robots, this is not the normal way of life for an individual. Despite, there are all types of emotions, which are necessary in all of our interactions because they communicate intentions and feelings. Decisions are sometimes made from the way we assess an event without even first asking questions.

46

Chapter 11 **Emotion Awareness**

The awareness of emotions alerts us to prepare for events that will provoke our peace of mind and disrupt our emotional stability. Frequently, when those situations occur we will take one of three routes - *pretend* nothing happened, *deal* with the situation, or *forget* about the encounter for the moment until later.

Our awareness of emotions will assist us in making decisions on how to respond and deal with events. It is very important to understand our emotions so that we are able to control them since they can become very intense as in anger and jealousy.

We may wonder where emotions came from. However, they are part of our lives and originate from our soul. They are from the affective domain of our being. If the individual does not know the self, how he or she feels, how to understand others and the way behaviours will affect the lives of others, there will be interpersonal conflicts.

Knowledge of the self will help the individual to regulate and control moods that will affect others. Each individual must be able to identify and describe *physiological* feelings [tightness in the stomach] *emotions* [humiliation], and *psychological* impulses [frustration] with the use of precise descriptive language.

Although some employees have experiences of stress, frustration, and anxiety, many cannot express those feelings. Instead, when adverse events take place, those persons mask or suppress feelings.

What is Emotional Awareness?

Emotional awareness is the ability to recognize and identify events that trigger certain feelings to make us respond. Awareness will make us reactive or proactive in our response to an event. Our emotions tell us what we should do in a time of impending danger or when we detect a negative behaviour from someone.

Emotions make us aware of what we feel, either after a recent encounter or from the past mixed with a new experience. The combination of past and present will bring on feelings of excitement, stress, or fear.

For instance, if the employee had a previous negative experience with a rude manager and he attacks again, whatever the result of the past might have been, that outcome might be the deciding factor for the choice of method to use in the new experience. The decision will determine whether the employee is to be cautious or impulsive.

Self-Awareness

Self-awareness is significant in deciding the type of reaction required for a particular incident. This means that, if the individual is cognizant of an approaching emotion, for example anger, the individual can make a decision for the appropriate response to prevent the situation from getting out of hand. He might think before speaking, or walk away until he is able to control his feelings.

The example of *Stacy* is evidence of emotional self-awareness and control. She sat at her desk mid-morning when her supervisor confronted her with a fist [*true*]. Trapped by fear and mixed emotions, she decided not to respond either verbally or physically. Eventually the supervisor returned to her office after banging the door behind her.

Here is a situation that could have erupted in serious outcomes if *Stacy* was not able to control her emotions. That was her last day on the job after years of emotional abuses from the supervisor. Obviously, the ability to recognize feelings, and to identify and manage them is one of the greatest social skills an individual will possess.

Emotional awareness and control are social skills to help in the effective management of workplace interpersonal conflicts.

Chapter 12 Understanding Emotions

The understanding of emotions is fundamental to successful leadership in any organization or group setting. This does not always happen because people can become impulsive and therefore, speak or act before asking questions. In any case, not only are people impulsive, but some individuals are very sensitive when spoken to with a loud tone of voice or if they are wrongly accused. For this reason those persons will react before asking questions.

Thoughts

Thoughts play the leading role in the kind of response we will give to incidents that might humiliate or frustrate us. Therefore, the assessment of the thought process assists in the decision of an event concerning how to respond whether negatively or positively. Moreover, the basis of the decision frequently depends on the individual's perception of the event. Furthermore, being able to alter one's viewpoint through careful conceptualization of an event, will give a different perspective on the cause for an event, thus preventing spontaneous reactions that might develop into interpersonal conflicts.

Generalizations

Many times interpersonal conflicts occur because of an individual's reckless reaction from the generalizations of behaviours due to the lack of proper analysis of an event. Usually, an immediate employer will make assumptions about an employee from historical events and behaviours or cultural and ethnic backgrounds. Admittedly, the manager ought to pay attention to the employees' interpersonal behaviours and performances. Nevertheless, no supervisor should make global assessment of outcomes, especially if he is the direct cause for problems. When those times occur, the manager is not fully aware of his emotions or he neglects to pay attention to situations resulting in anger and resentment from an employee. Making generalizations, means one size fits all.

Interpersonal Emotional Conflicts

The symptoms of emotional abusive situations are often hard to identify, explain, or express effectively for others to understand precisely what the other person feels. Furthermore, for the employee who works in a hostile environment, he is subject to various types of emotional reaction either from others or from personal feelings. Where there are situations such as aggression, manipulation, verbal abuse, and control, it would be difficult for employees who work in those environments not to react because of the discomforts they feel. Those situations result in psychosomatic symptoms sometimes resulting in headaches and distresses.

Hence, if the individual is not aware of his emotions, this lack of knowledge can result in interpersonal conflicts because responses will be according to feelings. This is where emotions and conflicts interface because the expression of emotions is in attitudes and behaviours.

It is important for the individual to be able to *name* the feeling precisely, and to *express* it with effective terms to bring out the intensity of the emotion being felt. For example, the feeling after an insult might bring about sadness, shame, embarrassment, humiliation, or anger. Perhaps, the individual will express the intensity of the emotion with descriptive terms such as *very, extremely, awful, terrible, and so on.*

Generally, interpersonal emotions are communicated by language, facial (Ortony, Clore, & Collins, 1988), and bodily expressions. According to Ekman, Friesen, & Arcoli, 2001, "the face provides information about whether an emotion is pleasant or not" (p.255). Conversely, there are also mechanical devices that are used to deal with emotions to take messages, telephone ID's to show which calls to accept and those to avoid, and the use of email messages.

Apprehension in Expressing Abuses

Apparently, emotional abuse is not one of those situations employees are willing to bring a complaint about. For example, a male employee who reports verbal abuse may refrain lest others think he is childish or feminine, while a female maybe called a crybaby. The danger is that if employees do not express their feelings from caustic diatribes or demeaning hurtful behaviours, a manager will continue doing so.

To illustrate, take the individual who has received an unfavourable review from a supervisor. If the report is undeserved, he must express his feelings to the supervisor. This is not always easy for some employees because a manager or supervisor might not entertain any confrontation. Moreover, it is not *always* that the employee sees the review.

In one situation, the employee had worked with the supervisor for over six years before seeing the negative reviews. Each year, she received the usual pep talk, and at the end of the meeting, she went on her merry way. This went on for all those years, until after an eventful situation she discovered that the employer was writing the most detestable and destructive things about her. She became emotionally ill for many months after the discovery.

The expression of emotions really has to do with the choices we make, our values, our expectations and interpretation of events, and our beliefs about the way those events should be. We respond according to the way we feel things should turn out for us. When this does not happen, we will respond in ways to show regret and or remorse. The apprehensive person will accept without question, and comply without fatigue.

Chapter 13 Conduct of Managers

If a manger or supervisor is skilled in emotional management, this will enhance effective problem solving; improved interpersonal relationships between colleagues and management; and in the decision-making process. Moreover, the behaviour of those who are in managerial positions is always on display before those whom they manage. Unquestionably, the positive behaviours of supervisors, managers, deans, professors, and administrators will create a working environment potentially conducive for effective interpersonal relationships.

The constructive behaviour patterns demonstrated by managers will motivate employees to produce, and this will change the paradigm from dissatisfaction to satisfaction because there is evidence of encouragement. In such an atmosphere, there are opportunities for personal growth and development, job enrichment, harmony, and increased productivity.

Very frequently, one hears from employees about the horrible state of a workplace. With careful thought, often the institution itself is not the direct cause, but the managers, supervisors, deans, and professors who make life difficult for employees. The main reason is that many of those persons spew their caustic emotional lava into the atmosphere affecting the employees in one way or another.

In one particular employment where the working conditions were extremely intolerable, the employees were constantly under pressure from management, including various interpersonal issues from certain objectionable colleagues. This atmosphere went on for years and those employees who complained were marked out for adverse repercussions. However, with the hiring of a new administrator, it did not take very long for the individual to influence the environment with positive behaviours, which gave each person the feeling of worth.

That experience was evidence of the impact one individual with a positive attitude had in an unhealthy working environment. It meant that employees had to change old behaviours and learn new ones, although this took some time in doing. The outcome after six months was tremendous. With each dissatisfaction, or negative reference to past injustices, the response was "How can *we* change the past to make things better for all of us?" Apparently, the manager with a positive feeling about the self can change an unhealthy working situation whether in the corporate or an educational institution.

When a manager is unable to manage his emotions, there will be interpersonal conflicts. The atmosphere will be charged with animosities and hostilities with each person simultaneously venting and protecting the self.

Those types of settings will create a claustrophobic emotional atmosphere causing pent-up anger and resentment to fester between manager and employees.

On any given day, people normally experience a variety of emotions ranging "from the quiet satisfaction of completing a relatively mundane task to the grief at the death of a loved one" (Ortony, Clore, & Collins, 1988, p.1; Tugade & Fredickson, 2002). Therefore, it is very important for the manager to understand emotions, and ensure he is able to control his own in a non-destructive manner.

The knowledge of one's emotions should help the individual become truthful in identifying needs, and appreciate the feelings of others. The reason is that emotions are "intra-personal internal reaction one has to an emotion-eliciting stimulus" (Guerrero, Andersen, & Trost, 1998, p.9).

Therefore, an emotion does not have to be expressed, even when the individual feels it. For example, an individual may feel angry about his employment situation, but refrains from expressing his feelings. The manager may feel like using negative words to a poor performance, but instead encourages the employee to try harder. This positive behaviour will gain respect and improve interpersonal relations in the workplace.

In addition, if a supervisor has the respect of those he manages because of positive behaviours they observe from him, there might be fewer *destructive* interpersonal conflict situations under his watch.

Moreover, a warm interpersonal working environment will create an atmosphere of camaraderie, rather than one filled will aggression, hostilities, dissatisfaction, dishonesty, and distrust. Everyone wants high regard and acceptance, instead of indifference, coldness, and insensitivity.

I would infer that most of the employee interpersonal conflicts originate from fear, control, managerial tactlessness, and hierarchical behaviours. Those situations seem to be most evident in the high-tech corporations and educational institutions.

Seemingly, when some individuals reach the pinnacle of their careers or profession, they pull up the ladder and lay it aside until when their fantasy collapses, and they slide down and fall flat on their faces. Evidently, the behaviour of a manager will enhance or destroy the workplace environment. It is his behaviour and treatment of employees, which seems critical for effective employee interpersonal relations.

Chapter 14   Functions of Emotions

Emotions are important internal mental structures, which are significant to life. The significance of emotions is vital because they bring awareness of an event to us, so that we can interpret and make decisions for appropriate action. This means an emotion such as fear will make us flee, or find some way of protecting ourselves from impending danger. It is the perception and intensity of the arousal, the awareness of the bodily changes such as trembling, or goose bumps that will make the individual take some kind of action for self-preservation. From the following, we understand the functions of emotions.

Signal Mechanisms

Further, "emotions are mechanisms whereby the organism signals to its cognitive and action systems that events are favourable or harmful to its ends," it would seem that it is the "ends that give the emotional event its emotional valence" (Lazarus & Lazarus, 1994, p.113). Therefore, if the emotion makes the individual feel aversion toward a specific event or object this will make him respond in a way that is appropriate to the feelings he is experiencing. This point clearly confirms the importance of knowledge about emotional awareness so that an individual can control his feelings, to decide how to respond. For the most part, people will react to perceived danger and this might increase heart rate. It means there is an unconscious learned behaviour of cowering before for example, an insensitive manager. The approach of the manager causes the body to pick up the signal of fear in reaction, resulting in the increased heart rate.

To Communicate Feelings

An emotion can communicate our intention much faster than words, and this influences the way others treat us due to our response to them and their behaviour towards us. They serve to communicate information about an event that will affect us in some way or another. For example, fear will signal to the observer that something has alarmed us, and this will motivate the individual to become curious and ask questions. Actually, we respond according to our perception of an event. We often become angry when someone has verbally abused us because we feel violated. The kinds of emotion we observe from someone will make us proceed with our approach or turn away from holding a conversation with the individual. Therefore, eye contact is fundamental in conversations, and so is active listening because they are indications of interest in the content and respect to the speaker.

To Express Rejection

Another point is that in the workplace, rejection occurs when a manager refuses to acknowledge the worth of an individual by constantly giving negative reviews on the

53

employee's performance with no particular merit to the allegations. In such a situation, the manager is communicating his feelings towards the employee. The employee in such a situation can offset the negative behaviour of the manager by countering a bad review if the individual believes in himself. Moreover, self-talk is vital to deal with rejection. This therapy will minimize the negative behaviours of a hateful person.[vii]

Warning Signals

As communication indicators, emotions function as warning signals telling someone he/she is not welcome through body language, and by failing to acknowledge the individual. They will also motivate behaviour either for protection from danger or for survival. For example, if an employee received a memo requesting a longer workday, he may not vocalize his thoughts. However, by his body language of open mouth and wide-eyes, these will communicate disappointment and even surprise. Another person may show contempt with a turned up lip, loud hiss, or shrugged shoulders. All those responses are reactions to a disagreeable event. In another situation, the individual may hide feelings of disappointment by smiling while he remains quiet with an uninterested attitude.

For Information

Emotions supply information to others through distinctive facial and vocal expressions and to one-self through distinctive thoughts and feelings (Clore, 1994, p.103). Facial cues give an indication of the type of emotion. For example, a smile tells the observer we are happy. In opposition, a sad look gives a completely different picture. Despite the evidence of facial expressions, non-verbal expressions give accurate information about the individual's attitude. As an information source, emotions will motivate an individual to action whether to change behaviour, or remain as is.

To Express Beliefs and Values

Individuals act according to what they *believe* and *feel*. Many people fear, not because of what they have experienced, but what might happen to them. When a supervisor bends over an employee's desk using threatening words, that person will feel fear and will either respond evenly or seek a way of escape from such an attack. Furthermore, when someone feels intimidated by another, he will become anxious and will even panic at the behaviour of the individual. Nevertheless, the individual may refrain from speaking up or putting up a defense because of fear or displaying forgiveness in response to religious beliefs.

Beth is a religious person quiet, very intelligent, and competent employee who works for Keith, her supervisor. Keith has a demanding attitude and tries to keep "Beth in line" because he feels intimidated by her. He has a professional degree with many years of service in the particular employment, but his interpersonal relationship is mediocre. For Beth, she goes to extreme lengths to please Keith. Although a professional herself, she is terrified of making a mistake because Keith embarrasses her in the presence of her colleagues. She lives in fear and is often tearful and irritable.

Assessment of Others

It is possible for an individual to change or modify emotions "during the course of an interaction" (Andersen & Guerrero, 1998, p.89). The reason is that emotions play a fundamental function with our assessment of others, and serve as the "basis on which we judge people" (Smith, 2002, p.115).

In Beth's situation, she might build up a clinical fear of Keith even when she knows that she has done her work efficiently. The lack of self-confidence will make her feel she cannot do anything right to please him. For this reason, she will be nervous and anxious even with Keith's infrequent approvals. Beth could change or modify her emotions by dealing with her fear of Keith.

In another situation, Connie worked for a bossy and domineering supervisor who stands behind her to watch her at work. Connie used to be extremely nervous and has often complained to her colleague about this intrusion and unprofessional behaviour. There came a day when the supervisor stood over her, so close that she could hear her breathing.

She found herself getting anxious as she hastened to complete the task. She suddenly said within herself, "Why am I allowing this person to do this to me. I will relax."

The self-talk helped her that day as she relaxed and put fear behind her. Here we see the cognitive [*positive thinking*] being used to cope with the emotion of fear, and the resulting change in behaviour. Connie became strong as she calmed down and dealt with the work. Fear in the workplace is a factor that may result in emotional problems for employees.

Understanding Behaviours

We use emotions to judge people in an attempt to understand their behaviours (Smith, 2002, p.111). Our we can also use our emotions to change our behaviours even when we have been hurt by another.

Tania's supervisor publicly reprimanded her soon after they arrived at work early one morning. This made her distressed and embarrassed because it happened several times during the particular week. Despite her usual quiet disposition, Tania decided to confront Basil who is her supervisor. However, before doing so, she confided her intentions to her colleague Ella, who informed her of a recent death in Basil's family. Although Tania was still annoyed, she thought about her plans, and decided not to pursue with her plans. Instead, she changed her behaviour and continued with her work as if nothing had happened. Clearly, the emotion of empathy seemed to have played a major role in the outcome of this incident because Tania changed the mode of response she had planned for Basil.

If Tania believed Basil reacted unprofessionally because of stress after a death in the family, she might ignore his rude behaviour and relate it to the recent loss. By ignoring her emotion, Tania will change her behaviour, due to her observation of Basil. On another occasion, she might have responded with an angry retort if she knew he had no reason to be disrespectful.

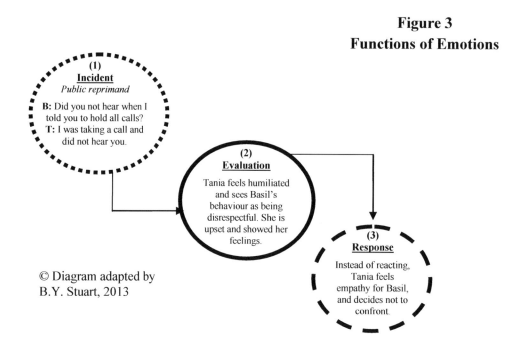

Figure 3
Functions of Emotions

In this example above, after hearing about Basil's loss, Tania's thoughts changed and this affected her behaviour towards him.

Chapter 15   Employee Emotional Abuse

Employee emotional abuse is not new, but "it has taken on a new feature with an environment of unending and relentless pressure due to increased competition and ineffective strategies for increasing competitiveness" (Bassman, 1999, p.4). This statement is extremely fitting for the current economic climate.

The fact that the job market is acute with increase unemployment and scarcity of jobs, working people, who are dissatisfied, miserable, frustrated, depressed, anxious, and unhappy with their jobs, usually have to work under severe emotional pressures because they do not want to become unemployed. Those symptoms are evidence of emotional abuse caused by the constant exploitation of their true feelings.

The act of emotional abuse is an imposition sometimes embedded unsuspectingly in the job description by employers, for their employees to follow for a variety of reasons. One way of describing employee emotional abuse is as if someone is daily walking delicately on the edge of sharp razors or on hot coals.

Each day that individual is in fear of making mistakes that will ignite the anger of a manager or supervisor. That anger can be in the form of verbal abuse such as unfounded blame, disrespect, criticisms, unreasonable demands, shame, open rebuke, and such like.

Individuals in those circumstances may have limited resources to express their emotions because they have to satisfy the demands of managerial personal insensitive preferences, and organizational goals.

In some situations, workers remain under those pressures because they have given years of contribution to the employment. Furthermore, some of them are close to retirement and do not want to start in a new place. For others, there are financial constraints and losing the job would jeopardize their ability to provide for their needs.

The most distressing factor about emotional abuse is that, the diagnosis is not easily detectable because there are no visible wounds. In spite of that, this type of abuse is just as damaging as any other because it affects the very soul of the individual. Those wounds have lasting effects years after the abuse is over.

One individual report fear of working in an office with others because of the experience of emotional abuse she suffered. Another one complained that she is always crying, but cannot give any reasons for feeling depressed even though she is no longer working with her adversary. Employee emotional abuse, strikes to the core of the individual's heart.

Mental Crime

Still, whatever the reasons for enduring those types of nervous tension, the results can be demoralizing and detrimental to health. Emotional abuse is a heinous mental crime against sincere, honest working people who *must* work to provide for themselves.

Succinctly described, emotional abuse is working in a pressure cooker environment of anxiety, strain, and worry of trying to please unscrupulous evil despots at all costs. They are tyrannical oppressors who do not care about the welfare of those who work for them.

Emotional abuse is mental pain and agony with many faces such as expecting more hours from an employee than was contracted. There are employees who experience violation of their rights, public reprimand, devaluing, and managers who show favouritism.

Another occasion for emotion abuse is the exertion of control with the use of performance appraisals and promotion opportunities.

This point was affirmed by Bassman, stating that, "a manager who uses power over a subordinate very likely will use performance assessment in an attempt to control the employee" (Bassman, 1992, p. xii).

For example, *Petunia* worked with a very controlling supervisor who did not acknowledge her educational abilities. She reported that this supervisor usually send threatening emails as warnings not to give her a fair review if she were "out of line."

The effect of those threats made her walk on eggshells and even took blame for things she did not do. Those were indicators of employee abuse. In some situations, employees feel fearfulness and powerlessness from the behaviours of insensitive supervisors.

Employee abuse is alive and kicking in a myriad of styles and ways. The intention is to destroy self-confidence, self-respect and to create stress. Furthermore, this type of abuse builds feelings of insecurity making the individual become obsessed with being perfect in an attempt to please and prevent criticisms from supervisors.

This kind of belief is a fallacy because it does not always work. The supervisor who makes an employee to feel this way is insensitive, and lacks empathy by placing the employee in a position of fear. Emotional abuse is a social crime.

Improper Use of Power

For the most part, the controller/manipulator uses power to commandeer the will of the employee who unconsciously thinks he is doing the right thing by not standing up for himself. Usually, the manager talks down to such an employee who, in some cases, because of that individual's personality is always at the receiving end for undeserved blame, punishment, and castigation. The improper use of power works effectively when the employee masks emotions of hurt to please an abuser.

Conflicts

When behaviours such as are described continue, they escalate into intra-psychic and interpersonal conflicts due to the discontent employees feel. Such conflicts whether expressed openly or covertly, affect the working relationships among employees.

Moreover, interpersonal conflicts result in a hostile working environment with animosities, lack of trust between employer and employee, and even among employees. Furthermore, if the improper behaviours of a supervisor remain unchecked, this will become the norm, and the employee will not expect any other type of behaviours from that individual.

In those situations, the employee endures mental stress, frustration, and humiliation for personal or other reasons, until there is an opportunity to change the situation.

It is obvious that employee abuse will thrive in a fertile unsociable and unprofessional soil, where there are spineless CEOs, and weak-minded educational administrators in educational institutions. Usually, the entire administration suffers because of the emotional crimes those individuals commit against their employees.

Emotional Labour

There is another form of emotional abuse identified as emotional labour. Hochschild (1983) describes emotional labour as "the management of feelings to create a publicly observable facial and bodily display."

Speaking as one who has experienced some dreadful work situations, this section describes emotional labour as employer prescriptive behaviour for the control of employees' emotions. It is what they expect from their employees.

Hochschild (1983) further added that emotional labour, is labour "which requires one to induce or suppress feelings in order to sustain the outward countenance that produces the proper state of mind in others."

She also noted that "this kind of labour calls for a coordination of mind, and feeling, and it sometimes draws on a source of self that we honour as deep and integral to our individuality" (p.7). Therefore, whether the employee receives insults from a customer, or is intimidated by the employer, that individual must accept such events as "part of the job" without complaints.

Another writer sees emotional labour as the behaviours of "employees whose jobs require them to manage their personal emotions in order to produce desired customer or client responses" (Krumel & Geddes, 2000).

There is confirmation to this report from many workers who have experienced this type of expectation in educational institutions and corporate working environments.

Devaluing Employees' Emotions

Ostensibly, "prescribed emotion norms might accompany nearly every social transaction as a primary means for the social control of minds" (Heise & Calhan, 1995, p.224).

If the employer expects the employee to behave according to an extrinsic model to present a false front from what he really feels, his emotion is being controlled and devalued.

To the casual observer, the employee becomes a robot or mechanical object, to dangle at policy-makers impulse and desires so that they can remain competitive at the expense of their employees' emotional health and well-being.

Hypothetically, this type of expectation incorporating the daily routine tasks, and one's personal life present a diagnosis of emotional abuse.

Chapter 16   Coping with Emotional Abuse

The report from researchers suggests that changes in the workplace have created a burden on workers who are expected to control their emotions even under very humiliating circumstances. In many workplaces, the treatment of workers is similar to machines that have no feelings. Those workers have to ignore their feelings in order to fulfill organizational and/or institutional goals, policies, and objectives.

Furthermore, the suppression of an emotion "is a form of monitoring and self-corrective action throughout an emotional event" (Gross & John, 2002, p.306). To control emotions means the employees have to mask their true feelings (Wharton & Erickson, 1993). This seems so evident in a time when the national economic state of events with bankruptcies, downsizing, and other situations make it difficult for the unemployed to obtain jobs.

Consequently, the employee acts not only in the interest of the employer, but also for himself by holding on to his position. Therefore, with job uncertainties, the employee has to find some way in which to cope in order to keep alert so that he can perform satisfactorily. This simulation of behaviour regulation in order to cope when dealing with emotions requires ongoing cognitive, behavioural, emotional, and physiological vigilance for the employee to be constantly on guard.

One can only assume that the impact on employees in such situations is tremendous, and there must be a considerable amount of stress-related outcomes. Heise & Calhan, 1995, (p.223), described this model of emotional expression by individuals stating that, "they intelligently guide their feelings and their displays of emotions to fit what is expected."

In an attempt to understand emotions, knowledge of the impact of emotions in conflict situations is important especially in the workplace because employees' emotions will influence organizational behaviour (Lazarus & Lazarus, 1994). Meaning depending on employees' response, managers will increase or reduce pressure on performance.

Coping with emotions refers to the "re-appraisal and avoidance of personal meaning" (Lazarus & Lazarus1994, p.159). One individual might dismiss a manager's insulting behaviour while another prioritizes it by dealing with the incident, e.g., the transferring of feelings onto a customer or colleague. Another individual might resort to emotional outbursts of anger or the taking of substances that are harmful instead of seeking resolutions to the problems.

Furthermore, the influence of emotions on conflict will stimulate an individual to take action resulting in outbursts of anger and disrespectful behaviours when there is violation of an expectation of a person's rights. Possibly, prescriptive behavioural scripts work best under those situations because each person tries to display behaviours, which are pleasing to the employer.

However, "when rules about how to feel and how to express feelings are set by management, and when workers have weaker rights to courtesy than customers do…what happens to the way a person relates to her feelings or to her face?" (Hochschild, 1983, p.89). The question asked here is, "Does the employer cares about the feelings of the employee?"

Transforming Emotions

The employee will cope with emotions by transforming them in the way he sees the world, and using those perceptions to interpret what he sees. Therefore, it is the appraisal, interpretation, and significance of the event that will motivate the individual to either cope with the emotion quietly or respond in a manner that satisfies him. For example, the uncertainty of one's position whatever the reason, will be the stimulus to induce the individual to seek for alternative employment or further training. The perception of the outcome of the loss of one's job and the impact of the emotions will be the operative factors to motivate for action (Planalp, 1999).

The intensity of an emotion will motivate an individual to act because of the way she feels about an insult or improper behaviour. The reason is that "when a superior acts inappropriately (and unjustly), this act triggers negative emotions, but the context of the social relationship also affects emotional responses and the likelihood of emotional expressions" (Johnson, Ford, Kaufman, 2000, p.130). Obviously, the response would depend on the strength and quality of the interpersonal relationship between the superior and the subordinate to influence a behaviour resulting from a violation.

Building Relationships

Furthermore, judgments are made of people by their behaviours, which will determine what will help to build relationships or keep individuals apart. In addition, one could even venture further by proposing that the response or non-response of an unpleasant remark depends on the personality of the recipient. For instance, an employee might cope by compromising, and accommodating an inappropriate behaviour from a superior or colleague because she wants to keep the relationship to remain intact.

Appraisal of an Event

An employee's evaluation of a superior or colleague's inappropriate behaviour may decide the possible outcome that will help to plan how she will cope with such an event in the future.

Consequently, appraising an event is really "an active exercise that makes us negotiate between our personal agendas, e.g., goals and beliefs and the characteristics of the environment e.g., the kind of person with whom we are interacting" (Lazarus & Lazarus 1994, p.144).

Therefore, after receiving an unfair appraisal from a supervisor, an employee might think of being aggressive, passive, or assertive. Furthermore, emotional actions are not limited to physical or overt expressions, but include various types of mental activities that prepare the individual for readiness to respond to physical actions or lead him to monitor others' opinions and to re-establish one's reputation (Parrott, 2002, p.346).

Methods for dealing with Workplace Abuse

Employee abuse results in emotional conflict and poor interpersonal relationships. The hurt employee might respond under mental and physiological strain caused by the repressed emotions and unfair treatment. Following are three response suggestions for dealing with workplace abuse:

Awareness

If there is evidence of abuse, the employee should pay attention to feelings, thoughts, and his/her physical state. In an incident that arouses emotions, the employee should take time to be composed, especially when anger is present. It is better to find some form of diversion for a while that will occupy and take the place of resentment and anger. Since it is not wise to repress feelings of hurt; therefore, talking with a trusted friend who will give support and advice is a good way to begin dealing with violations. *Always keep a journal.*

Confrontation

An aggrieved employee might not want to deal with problems because of fear. There might also be the concern of over-reacting causing the person to accept the abusive treatment without challenge in the hope that it will go away. This does not always happen. However, as soon as the individual can recognize an emotion that is the result of inhumane treatment, she should identify it and decide how she will deal with the behaviour. For example, if the superior speaks in an inferior manner and this makes the employee feels devalued, he or she must say so and be clear, honest, and specific about it. Lack of confrontation only perpetuates an insufferable situation from one individual that is causing pain to another person.

Intervention

An employee may choose not to confront the superior because she is paralyzed by fear, thinking that the individual will be reluctant to admit to the truth. "Emotions provoke deception and deception provoke emotions" (Buller & Burgoon, 1998, p.381). Evidently, "saving face and lying are deceptive methods used for avoiding to face the truth about a situation" (p.381). With the fear of the superior being dishonest, this gives rise to emotions of worry, skepticism, and lack of self-confidence. Therefore, if there is threat of deception and the employee is hesitant to face the superior alone, she should have a third person who is trusted, objective, and impartial. These factors should be present in any discussions concerning abuse.

The discussion in this book shows the many ways in which emotions and conflict are inter-related and their effect in the workplace to both the employee and the employer. It would be advisable that further research be carried out to find out how employers are addressing situations such as employee abuse and the effects of emotional conflict on employees.

There is no justification for any employee to be uncomfortable in the workplace if that person is performing duties in a professional and acceptable manner. These are concerns that need to be researched.

Table 1

<u>Effect of Emotional Abuse</u>

Communication Skills	Interpersonal Relationships	Behavioural/ Psychological
• Abruptness • Manipulative • Quarrelsome • Brusqueness • Aggressive • Argumentative • Difficult • Unmanageable	• Destructive behaviours • Shouting • Un-sociable • Lack of interaction • Picky • Cold • Angry outbursts • Intractable	• Obsessive behaviour • Tension • Fear • Anxiety • Frustration • Withdrawal • Depression • Feelings of rejection

Copyright © 2013 Table Adapted by B. Y. Stuart

Chapter 17 {style="float:left"}

Emotion Type {style="float:right"}

I included emotion type because we often hear someone say, "Oh, she is so emotional. I don't like to be around her." Yet, no one usually explains the *type* of emotion the individual is expressing. It would seem fair to ask what is wrong before assuming that the person is just being "emotional" over nothing. Seeing someone crying is only the result of what the individual is feeling. Crying does not tell the true story of what is really happening to the individual.

Admittedly, some people get over-reactive when unusual things happen in their lives. Others might take incidents in their strides and not make a big thing out of misfortunes. Obviously, when someone cries after an emotional experience, that person is expressing feelings from the pain of hurt. The individual who is crying is communicating to the observer that, "something is wrong with me." Rather than to ignore or shrug the shoulder by passing on the behaviour as insignificant, it would be important to find out *why* the individual is crying, and *what* can be done to bring the person back to a sense of calmness.

Emotions are *personal* subjective feelings which an individual has concerning an experience. For example, if after receiving an unfair review from a supervisor Jackie says, "I felt very badly about the things I read in the review concerning me." This explains disappointment and even sorrow depending on the reaction of the individual. The observer will also notice the body language because non-verbal reveals how the person is really feeling. What does the emotion reveal?

For example, does the individual express intense disappointment after reflection on the review. How deeply does the script of the review affect the person? In what ways does the review affect the individual? What types of emotions is the individual experiencing? How are those emotions affecting the individual?

Can she continue working calmly for the remainder of the day? Does she need support? Is she irritable, stressful, or tensed? The foregoing questions are important because emotional types give specific explanation about *how* the person feels, and describes precisely the *intensity* of the emotion.

In the above example, the assistant stated that she felt "very badly." It would be simple to say that the adjective before the adverb, emphasized the intensity of the feelings, but did Jackie express the true intensity of her feelings.

To only say, "feeling very badly" might be a casual off-handed reference with no expressed emotions. Still, if Jackie screwed up her face, knitted her brows, or pounded on her desk and said, "I was very disappointed," this would express intense passion concerning her feelings about the review.

Additionally, if Jackie was crying and her shoulders shook, that would certainly tell the onlooker more about how she felt about the disappointment. It would further express the influence of the observed emotions.

Again, would it be against the review itself, or the person who wrote it? Nevertheless, the identified emotion type and its intensity, whether the feelings were mild or severe at the time the incident occurred must be clearly explained.[viii]

The Role of Cognitions

The cognition of an emotion serves as an indication that something was pleasant or unpleasant, and this knowledge will influence behaviour. Those feelings result from the cognitions; that is, the imaginations and thoughts conjured up about the event.

The explanation concerning the severity and influence of an emotion is often in behavioural form. This could either be in the form of confrontation, distancing, or avoidance. Hence, showing the evidence to the interrelatedness of the affective, cognitive, psychological, physiological, and behaviour.

Our behaviour is the result of our cognitions of an event. Cognition is a process of mental activities whereby the individual is actively engaged in thinking in order to transform, expand, deduce, and store information to deal with other situations. Indeed, it is possible to use the learning from one situation to another on a similar occasion.

Schachter & Singer (2001) noted that, "cognitions arising from the immediate situation as interpreted by past experiences provide the framework within which one understands and labels his feelings" (p.77). Clearly then, one could infer that past infractions play a significant role in determining how one feels about a new incident from similar source.

Take for example, the illustration given above with the supervisor and the assistant. If the supervisor called the assistant into his office later, she might be hesitant about expressing warmth for fear of being disappointed again.

Consequently, cognitions are what we use to determine whether the state of physiological arousal such as goose bumps will be labeled as, for example, the result of "anger," "joy," "fear," etc., (Schachter & Singer, 2001, p.77).

With this data then, one can conclude that physiological arousal and cognitive factors are interrelated for identifying emotions. Unmistakably, the cognitions are the results of our thoughts and imaginations. It is from those that we make sense of what we feel after an event.

Returning to emotional type, although some researchers reported the complexities of emotions and the interrelatedness of cognitive, psychological and physiological, and behavioural processes, other researchers such as Ortony, Clore & Collins (1998) chose to ignore behavioural and physiological evidences.

They argued that those two evidences "concern the consequences or concomitants of emotional states, but not their origins" which, they "think are based largely upon the cognitive construal of events" (p.14).

Certainly, the way an individual appraises and understands an event or the behaviour of another, the outcome will help that person make sense of an emotion. The outcome of an appraisal will motivate the individual to be proactive, or reactive to an event.

Additionally, the outcome of an appraisal of an observed event will make the observer empathize when someone is hurting. That appraisal will also make the observer understand the emotion communicated by the hurt person, in order to be sincerely compassionate and sympathetic to the other person's pain.

The focus on the research by Ortony, Clore, & Collins was on "language and self-reports" to "specify different types of emotions," and "to construct a cognitive theory concerning the origins of the emotions" (p.14).

The researchers based their investigation on linguistic evidence that describes the type of emotion, and its effect on the individual. The premise is that "an emotion type is a distinct kind of emotion that can be realized in a variety of recognizably related forms" (p.15).

The assumption is that there are many ways to describe an emotional concept, depending on how the individual experience the event and the perception of the impact of the emotion. The example used by the researchers was the concept "fear" that can be manifested in varying degrees of intensity such as "concern," "fright," "petrified," and so on, (p.15).

They also noted that, "when fear becomes psychological it is expressed as anxiety." This research was very significant to mention in this book because it gives a different perspective on how an individual could describe an emotional experience, thus giving the listener a clearer understanding about an event.

In fact, a concise descriptive detail about an incident leads the effective listener into a critical thinking mode, as the person assimilates and reflects on the report given by the offended to describe subjective feelings.

An effective listener will ask pertinent questions to bring out details of the facts relating to the encounter, and the hurt person's feelings about the incident.

Furthermore, this type of listener will use three approaches to get to a clear understanding of the situation. *First*, he or she will ask about <u>precipitating incidents that created the event</u>. *Second*, the next question would relate to <u>how the hurt person reacted to the incident</u>.

Finally, the listener should ask <u>how the hurt person feels</u>, and what <u>course of action</u> he or she will take to make the situation better.

For example, if Jackie reports there had been previous problems with the supervisor that could have given rise to the poor review; this is an opportunity to ask more questions. What if her performance had not been satisfactory and this was an ongoing situation?

In contrast, there might have been personality differences whereby the supervisor did not like Jackie for whatever reasons. Clearly then, before passing judgments about any emotional situation it is imperative that one finds out more information in order to make a just assessment of the reason for an event.

Therefore, if Jackie said, "When I read the appraisal I was very disappointed," this gives the effective listener an opportunity to ask open-ended questions such as

"What do you mean by being 'very disappointed?'"

"Why were you disappointed?"

"Explain more to me", and so on.

Just saying that she was "very disappointed" would not be sufficient to justify how the person really felt or what caused her to receive a poor review.

Other emotions that could come out of "very disappointed" might be *"dissatisfied"*, *"saddened,"* and *"angry."*

Chapter 18 An Emotional Reaction

An emotional reaction is a response given to the awareness or influence of an emotion after an encounter. The event might make the individual feel happy or sad, angry or calm, anxious or relaxed, frightened or composed, impressed or embarrassed. For example, an unpleasant event might be one that brings on stress. A different event might result in fear that causes cold sweat to appear on the person's body. Importantly, an emotional reaction is the result of the prominence one gives to an incident after internal processing. The reaction will be preceded by the impact of the event on the individual and related factors that caused the situation. Moreover, it is the *interpretation* of the emotion that makes the individual decides how to respond to the event.

Depending on the interpretation, it will be the *significance* of the event to the individual that will bring about a particular type of response. Hence, the thoughts play a major role in the type of emotion that will result from an incident, and also the behaviour that will accompany the emotion. Once again we see the complexity and interrelatedness of cognitive, affective, and behaviour.

For example, a supervisor might threaten an employee with an unfavourable end of year review for unsatisfactory performance. The smart employee will think about the loss of promotion or an increase in salary. Therefore, that person will seek to improve the performance. Whether the unsatisfactory performance review was warranted or not it will be the deciding factor for the type of response from the employee to the manager, and motivation for improved performance.

Clearly, if the employee decides to take the manager's threat seriously by making adjustments to improve his performance, it might work to his advantage. This means that the employee has thought about the outcome [cognitive]; considers the loss of pay or even the position and feels some regret [affective]; and this results in change by doing better work [behaviour]. The employee might have been careless, maybe getting to work late, or wasting material. Whatever the reasons, it was his/her decision to make changes after the effect of the emotion of loss that might have incurred from the supervisor's threat. Since emotions influence the thought pattern, the result of the assessment of the threat, enhanced the decision relating to the type of behaviour that will be demonstrated as a response.

In another scene, the response could be reactive resulting in anger. The employee could have decided not to take responsibility for personal weaknesses and issue his/her own threat to the supervisor.

Besides, the result depends on various factors such as the ability to process information, differences of communication styles, cultural differences, poor problem solving skills, personality traits, introversion or extraversion, and the emotional health of the individual. Additionally, the culture and structure of the workplace will influence an emotional reaction by a hurt employee. Besides, the interaction of the processes of feelings, thinking, and response result in "the subjective experience of emotion, arousal, and overt behavioural expression."

Those "experiences and arousals are internal events, that are expressed in behavioural manifestations presumed to signal the internal events" (Buller & Burgoon, 1998). When we encounter an event, our body communicates how we feel, and our thoughts evaluate and appraise the situation (Lazarus & Lazarus, 1994).

The outcome from the appraisal will determine the type of response. That is, if we will react, where, and when. However, that decision might well be an impulsive one which often leads to consequences, if we allow harmful thoughts to control our emotions. The hypothesis is that when people allow faulty thoughts to occupy their minds, those thoughts will lead to impulsive emotional reactions.

Obviously, when an individual uses the cognitive processes effectively, that person will take time to evaluate, assess, reason out the pros and cons for actions, which might lead to better interpersonal relationships, especially in a working environment. That person will use problem-solving skills to arrive at answers, rather than jump to conclusions.

Usually, the insightful individual will use concepts such as "if", "then," "what," "why", "how", "who", "when', and "where" before making concrete decisions. This exercise is even more critical to those who hold supervisory and leadership positions. The person who goes through this exercise will be in a better position to avoid making arbitrary or unilateral decisions.

Furthermore, if senior managers and supervisors would take time to explain, teach, include, and guide employees there might well be less reactionary responses to their decisions.

When employees feel less important to the organization or institution, their reaction will be uncooperative, and they will only give so much, and no more. A feeling of satisfaction is vital to the morale of employees, mainly when supervisors demonstrate warm inclusive attitudes towards them. People will react to emotional coldness, similar to natural temperature. There will be withdrawal because of discomfort and even fear.

An individual responds to an emotion in a subjective manner due to the emotional outcome from an event. That person behaves according to personal experience, awareness, perception, and not someone else's.

In the example below **D** avoided **S** in the meeting because of her feelings of hurt and disappointment. Although her behaviour might seem unprofessional, or even childish one might say; yet this was *her* way of responding to what *she* interpreted to be dishonesty and unfair treatment. Ekman & Davidson (1994) emphasized that, "psychologically, emotions alter attention, shift certain behaviours, and activates memory." In addition, "physiologically," emotions "rapidly organize the responses of different biological systems including facial expression, voice, etc., that produce a bodily milieu that is optimal for effective response" (p.123). Consequently, even if the individual did not say anything, the body language alone will display dissatisfaction.

The case study below, illustrates the interrelationship and involvement of cognitive, affective, and behaviour in emotional reactions.

Case Study

Deidre has been Assistant to Sally for two years. Recently, the relationship was difficult with a "business as usual" understanding. The day in question, a folder with a very important report required for the weekly staff meeting was missing, but Deidre did not know about the folder. It is 40 minutes before the meeting begins, and here comes Sally to Deidre's desk.

Sally: may I have the folder with the report I gave you to copy this morning?

Deidre: [*taken by surprise*] asked, what folder? I do not recall receiving a folder from you. [*Heart pounding, because Sally is often very angry and accuses **D** of things she has no knowledge about*].

Sally [*looking flushed and impatient, accusingly said*], this morning I gave you a folder to make ten copies of the report for the meeting which is about to begin. Did you make the copies?

Deidre [*covertly angry and with emphasis responded with*] Sally, you did not give me that folder. [*Sally had a habit of forgetting things, which at times was to Deidre's advantage*].

Sally: [*angrily*] are you calling me a liar? You are an extremely difficult person to work with.

Deidre: [*trying very hard not to explode, tremblingly responded with*], I am not calling you *anything*. You did not give me the folder. You are constantly blaming me for your own mistakes. [After thinking she *calmly* suggested], Why not look on your desk to see if it is under the pile of papers? [*This calmness always irritated Sally and made her angry*]. [Deidre thought, *she is always talking down at me and making me out to be stupid*].

Sally: you *never* own up to your faults. I find your tone to be very rude and insolent [*as she angrily walked away*].

*After returning to her office, Sally checked her desk and found the folder hidden under a stack of papers. She did not apologize or inform Deidre that she had found the folder. Instead, **D** discovered this at the meeting. [She thought, "I am going to confront her after this meeting. She is so conceited, and always blaming me"].*

Deidre *feels depressed and unhappy. She is irritable and hates the way Sally talks down at her and makes her feel that she is incompetent. In her mind, she thinks Sally is manipulative and controlling, with a habit of reprimanding her for the least infraction whether she was at fault or not. Her life is miserable and stressful. Most times Sally did not explain herself properly, and this resulted in misunderstandings. At other times, she would forget to give instructions to Deidre and would later accuse her for her own mistakes and lack of proper communication. Deidre hates going into work as each day becomes more frustrating and filled with tension. She is thinking of resigning or finding another position.*

In the example given above from a real life situation, Figure 3, below explains the relationship of emotions [*affective*], action [*behaviour*], and thinking [*cognitive*] that bring about reactions to events.

From this example, many factors are evident pointing out the complexities of emotions from the point of view of controlling them without reacting impulsively or unsociably. Evidently, the factors of cognitions, feelings, and behaviour interact to bring about a response that can be reactive or proactive.

The example from the point of view of **D,** reflects her discontentment and unhappiness regarding the interpersonal relationship with her **S**.

Obviously, after thinking things over, **D** decides to confront **S**. This would seem to be a proactive response to discuss the unhealthy work relationship. Still, was it?

Figure 4 (a)
An Emotional Reaction

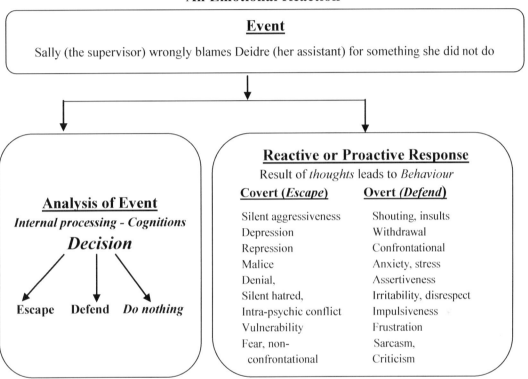

©2013 Diagram Adapted by B. Y. Stuart

Figure 4(b)

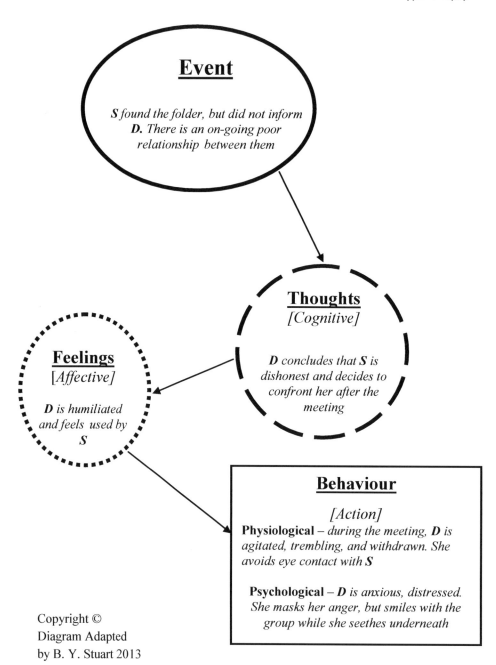

Event

S found the folder, but did not inform D. There is an on-going poor relationship between them

Thoughts
[Cognitive]

D concludes that S is dishonest and decides to confront her after the meeting

Feelings
[Affective]

D is humiliated and feels used by S

Behaviour

[Action]
Physiological – *during the meeting, D is agitated, trembling, and withdrawn. She avoids eye contact with S*

Psychological – *D is anxious, distressed. She masks her anger, but smiles with the group while she seethes underneath*

Table 2

Event

The event may be an encounter, e.g., verbal with a manager or supervisor that produces emotional stimuli resulting in painful *feelings*. Those feelings will come from the cognitions of the internal processing. There will be some type of reaction from the injured individual; whether covert or overt.

It is the *awareness* of the emotion from the encounter that will result in a reaction to make the individual withdraw or attack. However, some type of cognitive appraisal concerning the encounter will take place in order to guide the decision for response. Otherwise, the individual will act impulsively, or ignore the emotion.

Essentially, after awareness it is the *interpretation* and *significance* of the encounter that will enhance the decision for response. If the response is overt, it will communicate to the other person that the victim is not pleased. Else, the offended will mask the hurt, and maybe deal with it later.

The response will either be *behavioural*: raised eyebrows, withdrawal; *psychological*: anxiety, stress, frustration, irritability; and *physiological*; .increased heart beat; goose bumps; and increased perspiration.

©2013 Diagram Adapted by B. Y. Stuart

Table 3

Emotions (*Feelings*)	**Cognitive (*Thinking*)**
In order to have a complete awareness of feelings, the individual must be able to, *acknowledge*, *identify*, and *reflect* on the type of emotion experienced. Moreover, feelings must be expressed in terms that give a clear and concise description of the experience. There must be an explanation of the intensity of the emotion, e.g., "I was *very* embarrassed" as opposed to "I was embarrassed."	The thoughts occupy cognitive processes that can affect the behaviour after an appraisal of an event. The appraisal comes after acknowledgment of the event, and the emotion that resulted. Thoughts about our emotions [feelings], whether positive or negative, will help us to decide the *cause* for our feelings about an event. ***D's*** feelings of frustration and disappointment led her to believe that ***S*** is dishonest for concealing information. ***S's*** behaviour and perhaps past infractions against ***D*** may have caused her to make the decision to confront.

Behaviour

D's feelings, and the result from the outcome of her appraisal of the event, will determine her behaviour. It will motivate her to take some type of action to counter what she perceives as ***S's*** dishonesty.

Chapter 19   Emotions and Health

The emotional state of every worker is very important because it enhances performance and maintains or affects health. The reason is that, whether for good or ill, our emotions influence our health (Lazarus & Lazarus, 1994, p.39). Evidently, if the workplace is conducive to effective interpersonal interactions, we can expect workers who are happy, responsive, productive, when there is camaraderie among them. There will be less absences and employees and employer will experience togetherness and cooperation.

When we speak of emotional health, most of this has to do with the thoughts that occupy our minds. In a working environment, those thoughts can originate from the stipulations and expectations of employers from their employees. Some of those requirements are often outrageous, and employees may have to comply with unreasonable demands that are not humanly possible on a daily basis.

It does not matter how well adjusted an individual might be, with a continuous bombardment of unfair treatment, that person might eventually break. Still, the individual who is able to maintain continuous composure from verbal abuse is doing so under great emotional strain.

One of the ways people can secure emotional health is by thinking positive and realistic thoughts. There are also times when they will have to do some self-talk to encourage themselves. For example, when a supervisor tells an assistant "I can't trust you to do anything right," this is very hurtful.

What the supervisor is actually saying is that the individual is incompetent and incapable of doing anything right. However, if the assistant banishes the thoughts of incompetence and see herself with equal ability; as she goes on her way, this attitude will counter the effects of the injury the supervisor intended.

Janice worked with a dean for a few years. At the initial stage of their meeting, it did not take many months for her to discover that it was not a good fit. Nevertheless, after many complaints and painful experiences she decided to ignore her supervisor Alana. One day after humiliating Janice and wrongly accusing her, Alana observed, "You are always so calm" because Janice did not respond to her verbal assault.

According to Janice, that was the only way "I could deal with the open rudeness and constant blame I received from Alana."

Obviously, Alana did everything to have a confrontation with this employee. After years of abuse there came another day when Janice confronted her and asked, "Why do you always give me a hard time? What have I done to you? I am human with feelings just like you." Apparently, that did not go down very well and Alana approached Janice with her fist ready to strike her.

Again, Janice was in control, and with fear and nervousness tried to talk sense into Alana. It turned out that Janice had come to the end of the road with her supervisor, and that was the last day she worked at that institution. She literally ran from her job because of fear and no recourse for the constant abuse.

One could make an assumed guess that Janice must have been frightened for her life when she saw the fist coming at her. Fortunately, her "guardian angel" was watching over her that day, and she finally escaped the wrath of a cruel employer's bad temper. In her own words:

> I sat at my desk and watched the size of the fist that was about to strike me, I feared, but not could let Alana know how I felt because I was scared for my life. The only exit was right in her path. Even then, I just could not move because I was so petrified, and glued to the chair with fear. I am sure God spared my life that day because Alana could have pulverized me. I would have been minced meat, with no witnesses to speak on my behalf. I thank God for being with me that day. It is not an experience I would wish on anyone. My life was spared that day, but we have heard of other situations where employees lost their lives on the job at the hands of others.

When employees work with individuals who are unable to control their emotions, there is the probability that everyone might be at risk. No one knows when that person will become angry and put the lives of others in danger. Life presents all kinds of problems, but some people tend to transfer those problems onto others when they become over-bearing. For some individuals, they are unconcerned about how their behaviours affect others, and so they express their feelings, without thought for anyone.

The way people behave in a crisis usually express their emotional health when something goes wrong. They might be the first to become angry over little things that could have been blown over. Those persons allow their emotions to take control and they say and do the wrong things, which later make them ashamed. People must understand that they are responsible for their own behaviours, and saying "I am sorry too many times" will become redundant because after a while it does not work.

Nobody wants to be around individuals who cannot control their emotions. Those persons display emotions of anxiety, anger, worry, and even express feelings of low self-esteem. They put themselves down and allow their negative thoughts to overcome them.

On another note, since in many corporate and educational establishments employees may have to follow scripted programs to respond to uncomfortable verbal situations, especially from customers, there is the likelihood that those individuals will suffer some type of health problems when they have to suppress their emotions.

Including the unreasonable emotional response expectations, some employees have to attend training, deal with stringent policies, and in some situations with heavy workloads. If those employees do not carry out the desires of the employer, one can only assume that non-compliance results in emotional stress. Some have suffered from insomnia and others had to take anti-depressants to help them cope with uncomfortable workplace situations.

Sheila found herself waking up in the wee hours of the morning and unable to go back to sleep. She would lie awake thinking how she will face the supervisor the next day.

Another employee reported that just the thought of going into the office was burdensome, but at the end of the day, it was if "*I had been let out of a pressure cooker. Every evening I would race out of the office, happy to be away from the environment. There was such a burst of relief similar to a pressure cooker or balloon with the air slowing releasing air soon as I got on the train.*"

When employees have to work in such conditions, they cannot think properly in order to display the right emotions. It is amazing that many do not lose their minds under such strains. Still, we do not know the results of the outcome of those people who worked under those conditions.

When people have to work against the odds of losing promotion, and in some cases losing their jobs this is a form of emotional blackmail because if the employee fails to please the employer the job is at stake, one way, or another. Those types of situations are associated with emotional and psychological distress. These occur because employees become targets for emotional abuse from employers' agents such as cruel managers, clients, deans, professors, and students who disrespect them.

When incidents arise, the employee often has no recourse for action. In one situation, an assistant was told, "you must take any kind of behaviour from the students." That was not all, the supervisor said further "when I make a mistake you ought to own up to it to save my face." This may sound unreal. However, these situations do take place, and they will impinge on the emotional health of employees.

I cannot see the legality or legitimacy of forcing someone to accept behaviours that are offensive, harsh, and intimidating. Trying to keep up to the demands of any job is enough, than to encourage situations resulting in frustration and stress for an individual. There was a situation where an employee was new to the position, with no one to teach the individual about the job.

Obviously, this negligence resulted in many mistakes. Those errors caused the employee embarrassment from verbal attacks and harassment from clients, and constant put-downs from the supervisor who should have been empathetic.

Although I do not have statistical reports to cite, I believe there are many employees who have had to learn a new job by themselves through trial and error. Reports from employees and my own observation have shown that many educational institutions, and corporate employers do not teach new employees details about a new job, and therefore mistakes become part of the daily menu.

What is most disappointing is that when those mistakes occur, innocent individuals suffer because they get the blame for delays or the breakdown of equipment. Those conditions place pressure to bear on the employees making them exasperated and anxious.

Moreover, in such a setting employees will overlook intimidation and harsh treatment in order to hold on to a job. Matters only get worse when the instigator of control makes it his or her duty to use power or punishment to control the victim.

On another note, if there is no viable source for making complaints, the target suppresses the treatment, and it becomes institutionalized in the environment as the emotional distress becomes clinical to the individual.

The activity of holding back feelings will put strain on the nerves of the individual making that person become tensed and depressed. Furthermore, after a while the individual becomes adapted to inhumane treatment. An individual states, that she has become a sponge after years of emotional abuse from an employer in an institution of higher education.

Another one in the corporate area said, "I just cannot take it anymore. I must either resign or lose my cool." Employee emotional abuse is not a joke: it is reality. One can infer that on a daily basis, there are people who receive constant assault with insinuations and verbal abuse from insensitive, unqualified evil persons who are in managerial positions for which they do not deserve.

Five major factors in the workplace that could result in health situations include *work-related stress, employee exploitation, unfair treatment, poor managerial skills*, and *institutional abuse*.

Chapter 20   Managing Emotions

The management of emotion means that an individual has the ability to display sociably acceptable behaviours in the working environment. This skill is fundamental to the success of effective interpersonal relationships. The reason is that, when the individual is aware of the emotional situations that will affect his or her feelings in a negative or destructive manner, that person can control the response that will emanate from the emotion.

Clearly, if by controlling the emotions will make the individual responds in a positive manner, this will deflect the onset of a conflict situation that could have been emotionally destructive.

However, the acquisition of emotional management skills should not be for the purpose of avoiding punishment or receiving rewards, but for personal development for both supervisors and their assistants. The management of emotions takes time and effort, and people who do not attempt to learn how to manage their emotions use their behaviours as an excuse by placing a negative behaviour on the emotion (Planalp, 1999, p.3).

For instance, when someone becomes angry and say hurtful things to another person, then later makes an excuse such as "Oh I do not know what came over me, it must be the weather." Obviously, that individual is using the weather to brush off a negative behaviour that might have caused emotional pain to someone else.

Although emotion "refer to the actual experience of feelings in a situation" (Johnson, Ford, & Kaufman, 2000, p.108), the individual should not allow feelings of anger and resentment to get out of control. Instead, that person should try to manage emotions in ways that are beneficial or suitable for the self and others.

Positive Reinforcement

Still, learning the skills for emotion management can come from various models of behaviour. For example, when an employee completes a project on time and the supervisor acknowledges and appreciates the effort made to get the work done, there should be recognition so that there will be a repetition of the same behaviour. Behaviourists call this model positive reinforcement (See Sarason & Sarason, 1996). Conversely, when employees feel unappreciated, there is often the temptation to react according to their feelings. This is where the management of emotion plays a vital role in the workplace. While it is true that the employee has an obligation to give the prescribed number of hours, for some people appreciation is as important as monetary compensation.

Modeling

Another approach for the learning of emotion management is modeling. If a supervisor models correct responses in critical emotional situations, that person is teaching the employees how to control their emotions without using destructive behaviours or hurtful language.

Besides, many of our learning experiences come from the environment from other people's behaviour. Hence, if the supervisor shouts at the assistant, he can expect to receive the same returned to him unless the other person is in control of his or her emotions.

Emotion management is vital for a conducive and amicable working environment. Each person in a team must be aware of, and understand his or her own emotions before trying to help other individuals with theirs. The acquisition of emotional skills, gives one the ability to deal with feelings without becoming destructive and obnoxious to other members in a team. That person must be in control of personal fears, anxieties, and anger.

Therefore, being true to the self about personal weaknesses and foibles is fundamental for modeling positive behaviours. According to Shakespeare "...above all, - to thine own self be true..."[1]

In addition, the individual must move away from the perception of the self in order to understand other peoples' feelings, and their way of dealing with conflict. This is important because the knowledge of how other people behave in a conflict situation will give some level of protection from possible impending danger. Obviously, if we know what will elicit an emotion in ourselves and in another person, we will demonstrate effective emotional responses to avert destructive behaviours that will create interpersonal conflicts.

Constructive Thinking

Moreover, in order to manage our emotions effectively, there are times when an individual has to develop positive thinking processes that will evoke the right emotion for constructive response. When someone is aware of angry feelings coming on, that person should not give way to the emotion. Instead, the feeling should be re-redirected to finding out the cause for the anger, and decide how he will deal with it. Allowing feelings to get out of control will not solve problems. Frequently, they only escalate the process of interpersonal conflicts that can become destructive most of the times.

It is natural to be angry when there have been open insults and wrongful blame. However, none of those situations should be cause for destructive behaviours because they do not solve problems. Rather, they complicate and increase problems. Essentially, when there are

---

[1] From William Shakespeare, *Hamlet: The Complete Works*. (Dorsett Press, NY, 1988), Act I. Scene III. Line 75:p.676.

identifiable issues between individuals in the workplace, they should be taken care of immediately to improve relationships.

Frequently, destructive behaviours originate from the cognitive processes that are sometimes inaccurate. If we do not think the correct thoughts in our analysis and evaluation of an event, we will have destructive outcomes. Those outcomes will make us ignore, avoid, or compromise in an attempt to deal with problems. Sometimes we have the wrong information about an event. We then take the faulty data to contrive responses that bring about destructive, unsociable, and unprofessional behaviours. Consequently, the collaboration of thought, emotion, and reaction are essential for the effective management of emotion to display the correct sociable responses.

Experiential learning

One of the ways in which supervisors and managers can model behaviours, is through experiential learning when they detect the types of behaviours that bring about effective or ineffective employee responses. Experiential learning of personal behaviours will help to give the managers sensitivity to the feelings of others, and prepare them for any emotional reactions.

Furthermore, the history of earlier events should enhance the approach that will give the response expected from the employee. Historical events will assist the supervisor in selecting concepts and ideas from positive behaviours, to replicate and assist in interactions with the employees and in the decision-making process. When employer and employee have a good rapport with each other, there will be openness for explanations, self-expressions, questioning, and receptiveness.

In an open climate, people are willing to learn and to offer ideas because they know that they will be valued. Unfortunately, in some situations it seems that supervisors are unaware that when employees receive positive treatment, it is to the advantage of the employer.

Understandably, that might be so, but the fact remains that both employer and employee need each other, and a wise employer will implement strategies to maintain harmony with his employees. Nevertheless, it is impossible to teach someone the management of emotion if the teacher does not know how to manage his own. First, the individual must be able to identify and own his emotions before even attempting to decide on the correct skills for management.

Learning comes from experience either practically or through theory. Therefore, if an individual does not know how to react to certain situations, how can he teach another how to behave in similar ones?

Moreover, the way some people manage their own emotions is by fears or threats from other people. Those individuals allow exterior stimuli to control them and they cannot select or apply effective skills to deal with emotional situations.

Furthermore, some people have not developed qualities of self-control, patience, kindness, tolerance and such like to deal with problems. Instead, they allow their feelings to control the interpersonal situations that come into their lives.

Others allow people who use manipulative tactics to control them so that they are unable to think out solutions for the least interpersonal problems. The dependence on others to solve problems will eventually make an individual become a robot, unable to think or use personal judgments in critical situations.

The individual who uses negative emotion as an excuse to deal with problems will eventually put blame on another person for displays of emotional outbursts. Those expressive bursts of emotions will affect others who are around the emotive individual because emotions are transferable due to their "social nature" (Parrott, 2001, p.1).

When Stella came out of Dally-Ann's (her supervisor) office, she was visibly shaken with tears streaming down her face. Florrie went over to give support and she started crying too. Some emotions are infectious like yawning, when one person starts, others are often affected.

When emotions are not effectively managed, they will eventually lead to behavioural problems that are often unsociable. Those behaviours can also create low self-esteem when others avoid being around the individual. Unrestrained emotions cause interpersonal conflicts. Each person should learn how to control his or her emotions from experiential situations. It is from those experiences skills are developed, after reflective thinking, and conceptualization of what is acceptable and what is not.

For example, Sally asked Jill to order legal paper for a project. In Jill's mind, she thought Sally meant yellow lined paper and so she placed an order for what she thought. It turned out to be the wrong kind.

On reflection, Jill recalled that this was not the first time Sally did not express herself clearly to her. Jill took a proactive action and asked Sally to send her an email of exactly what she wants in future to avoid mistakes.

In this example given above Jill learned from her experience with Sally that she did not give accurate information and therefore, there were occasional mistakes. By taking the correct action, she avoided the occurrence of a conflict that would certainly have happened if she had behaved differently. Experiential learning plays a major role in the management of emotions.

If our emotions become uncontrollable, this will lead to interpersonal conflicts. In a workplace setting, any negative behaviour will create animosities and hostilities among employees at all levels. Nevertheless, the management of emotions takes time and effort to learn appropriate skills, which are socially acceptable. According to Planalp (1999), "one way to manage feelings is to manage the attention given to the eliciting event or to the feelings themselves" (p.78). This is very true because the emotional feeling usually depends on the outcome of the appraisal of an event, and the resulting feeling that accompanies the evaluation.

Furthermore, the management of emotional events depends on the evaluation of the event, communication, factors determining the event, the impact of the event, the history of the event, perception of the event, re-appraisal of the event, and the problem solving skills of the individual in a conflict situation.

Experiential events will help us to select some type of responses that are either negative or positive that will be professionally and sociably acceptable or unacceptable. Still, for a response to be positive and effective the individual must process, analyze, and reflect in order to make the right decision for application. In that process he or she will think over what worked the time before, the effect of the response, and whether it is wise to use it again.

Often, the experience of a past infringement will motivate an employee to seek for some kind of resolution. This could be confrontation, or seeking out a third party. The awareness of our emotions helps us to control them so that they do not control us to cause embarrassment and destructive behaviours.

Evaluation of the Event

Since emotions occur when expectations are violated (Planalp, 1999), a disappointing event will create some kind of emotional outcome, whether expressive or otherwise. The outcome will depend on how the person perceives the disappointment and what that violation means. Consequently, there must be effective processing, evaluation, and elimination before making decisions to arrive at a conclusive reason to find out why the violation took place. Hence, the outcome of the appraisal of the event will either evoke or resolve conflict.

Communication

It is very important that employees express their emotions when something upsets them.[ix] No one should cover up emotions with pretense or fear because this will only prolong negative behaviours. The reason is that "explaining and discussing an event helps because one is able to share with others and see another perspective" (Planalp, 1999). Furthermore, communication helps the hurt person to "step in and out of the experience" making him "both the subject and the object of the event" (Planalp, 1999, p.111). If the offender sees a negative behaviour, that person might emulate it, and the cycle will continue non-stop causing misunderstandings, frustrations, stress, and depression. In addition, Planalp (1999) intimated that "complaining and blaming oneself is not good." Therefore, "the experience must be confronted."

Factors Determining the Event

We respond to events according to where we are, who is involved, the type of event, and the time the event took place. However, it is easy for an individual to transfer feelings from home to work and vice versa. I believe that often, it is the transferal of other events that have nothing to do with work, that cause interpersonal problems.

Determining the Impact of the Event

One important factor to take into consideration is the impact of an event on the individual because this will influence the way he or she manages the emotional feeling. The way in which this is decided depends "on the attention that is given to the eliciting event or to the feelings themselves" (Planalp, 1999, p.78). Even if the force of the event is extremely crushing, the person can be distracted to take his mind off the event that triggered the emotions. That person can also be encouraged to remove from the vicinity when the emotion is intense and overwhelming. There are times when the very impact of the situation will cause the individual to become extremely angry and tensed.

Determining the History of the Event

The individual will recall the history of a past emotional experience (Wollheim, 1999). For example, if the employee knows what will make the supervisor angry, that person will avoid certain behaviours that will evoke an emotive response, e.g., outbursts of anger, or receiving a poor performance review.

Perception of the Event

Another example of managing emotions is the way an individual perceives the event (Planalp, 1999, p.79). The awareness and understanding of the situation will make the individual decide to move away from something that will be provocative to him. Furthermore, the individual distinguishes, identify, and discriminate things that are important to him in order to ignore those that are of lesser importance.

Re-appraisal of the Event

Individuals learn to manage emotional events by "changing the personal meaning of what happened by re-appraising them in a more benign and less threatening way" (Lazarus & Lazarus, 1994, p.159). For example, the employee who has to control his emotion using a prescriptive model from an employer might overlook a rude customer or an inappropriate behaviour from the supervisor by excusing the event with "he is probably having a bad day." Nevertheless, despite how the offended feels about the offender "the reality of the event must not be ignored as this would be denial" (Lazarus & Lazarus, 1994, p.160).

86

Chapter 21   Emotional Responses

Emotional responses are sets of behaviours that can act as defense mechanisms in order to deflect feelings of hurt and embarrassment. For example, stress and frustration can be the results of internalized anger from mistreatment. When feelings are internalized this affect the individual and cause psychological problems which can lead to depression and psychosomatic disorders. The assumption is that every day people face both negative and positive events; and those situations influence their emotion and physical well-being (Tugade & Fredrickson, 2002). Since emotions play an integral role in the daily life of individuals, it is important that everyone understands them. Therefore, knowledge of emotions is important to be able to process emotional information accurately and efficiently in order to solve problems, make plans, and achieve in one's life (Tugade & Fredrickson, 2002, (cited Salovey & Mayer, 1989-1990).

Although emotions are significant to our lives for protection and communication, this does not mean that the display of emotions should be indiscriminate. Similar to other life-situations there is always a right way, time, and place to express the way we feel without causing offense to others. Still, this rule is usually forgotten when someone is hurt, and that person responds according to personal feelings.

Whether an event is the result of environmental or personal stimuli, emotional responses can be in the form of panic – leading to anxiety or calmness either from the individual or from the support of other individuals. Additionally, the expression of emotion can be antisocial behaviours expressed in anger, insults, or loud outbursts.

Non-verbal Responses

Studies have reported that an individual's ability to understand general non-verbal behaviour predicts a range of workplace outcomes (Effenbein, Marsh & Ambudy, 2002, p.48). Admittedly, non-verbal behaviours are more accurate than verbal communication because of evident cues. One sees a tight fist, a frown, a smile, inattentiveness, and so on, which are cues for the observer to evaluate and decide what action to take, whether to approach or escape. However, emotional cues in response to conflict are regulatory devices, depending on one's personal goals in a situation (Gross & John, 2002). For example, an individual can change his tone of voice to deflect anger. In addition, facial expression can change from a frown to a smile, or the closed fist to openness for a handshake. This means that outward emotional response can be situational because of their regulatory ability.

The assumption is that "emotions are multi-componential processes that involve changes in subjective experience, expressive behaviour, and physiological responding" (Gross & John, 2002, pp.300-301). Therefore, regulation or change of emotions is a form of response to conflict situations that can serve a vital purpose in workplace situations. In such an instance, change can take the form of suppression, change of behaviour, and or change of cognitive thinking. The question here is, "What factors would motivate the individual to change his behaviour?" Those factors include the following:

Integrative Settings

The workplace is an environment where there are many differences in culture, personalities, opinions, likes, and dislikes. There are gender clashes, educational and economic differences, and even language differences. In such a setting, one will find many situations that will bring about distresses, and discomforts. There will also be feelings of rejection and inclusion, failures and successes, satisfaction and disagreements. These are some of the environmental situations found in the workplace. Consequently, since there are so many personality differences in such an integrated setting, emotional intelligence plays a vital role if individuals know how and when to express their emotions.

Emotional Intelligence

Emotional intelligence [EI] is helpful for reaching out to others in an effort to offer effective emotional skills such as care giving, listening, empathy, and modeling acceptable emotions to resolve conflict (Caruso & Wolfe, 2001]. The individual who is equipped with a set of emotional intelligence skills is better able to identify and control emotions. If someone can deal with issues rather than attack an individual, this I believe is an excellent spirit that will avert interpersonal situations in a working environment.

Furthermore, according to Matthew, Zeidner & Roberts 2002, in order, "to help others manage their emotions, it is crucial to keep one's own emotional perspective." This means that the supporter must know how to "calm an out-of-control person, be a supportive listener, and help with goal planning and implementation" (p.475). These are significant requirements for both employer and employee.

Besides, emotional intelligence requires conflict management and mediation skills that will be effective in helping to diffuse disputes in a working relationship. Knowledge of mediation processes will assist in the mending of broken communication in an effort to re-build a relationship. The mediator acts as a facilitator who is non-judgmental, listens objectively, and helps the parties settle their differences.

In addition, there are many other ways in which EI can be useful and some of these include career development and selection, specification of job description, assessment tool, evaluation, and recommendations (Caruso & Wolfe, 2001, pp.153-155).

Preliminary Appraisal of an Event

An appraisal is an assessment of how present circumstances influence one's goals and well-being, though not with the understanding of the need for deliberate, verbal, or symbolic factors (Parrott, 2002). Instead, an appraisal is concerned with the personal significance of an event, action, or object, rather than general information about it (Parrott, 2002, p.342). For example, when something important happens to an individual a high level of cognitive performance takes place. The individual might suppress the event after monitoring, and will eventually employ self-corrective measures to change his behaviour in an emotional event (Gross & John, 2002, p.306).

Re-appraisal of an Event

The re-appraisal of an event is an ongoing cognitive process. It involves cognitively transforming a potentially emotion-elicit situation to understand the meaning and make decisions on how to respond to an event. Reappraisal takes the form of leading an individual to re-construe the event in less emotional terms that will lead to decreases in emotional experiences, expressive behaviour, and physiological responding (Gross & John, 2002).

This argument leads one to infer that the way an individual interprets an emotional state depends on the cognitive understanding of that emotion. For example, the employee who constantly receives harassment from a manager may interpret the behaviour as cue to either do something about the negative behaviour or seek for alternative employment.

Besides, where an employee finds that he is underemployed this should be an indication to motivate him to seek for a more satisfying position. It will be the emotional dissatisfaction or an unpleasant working environment that will be the emotional stimuli to make an individual take action.

Positive Emotional Responses

Proactive responses will influence empathy and compassion. One way in which this is expressed, is to reflect back to the speaker what was said to bring out feelings. Another way is if a colleague is crying after an unfair treatment by a supervisor, another one might try to offer support to the hurt person. The supportive person reflects on the hurt individual's feelings of pain and responds accordingly. In such a situation, it is the impact of the emotional event that will make the consoler take action.

Nevertheless, positive emotional responses are not associated with specific problems needing solutions. Instead, they "broaden attention and create situations where cognitive, physical, and social resources can be built" (Lord & Kanfer 2002 (cited Fredrickson, 1998)). The writers gave an example that "joy promotes play, which helps to build physical, social, and intellectual skills.

Additionally, "contentment broadens the self and worldview and creates the urge to integrate; love triggers positive emotions and solidifies individual and social resources" pp.10-11. Most likely, positive emotional responses will create effective social relations because they serve as buffers to the "harmful physiological and cognitive effects of negative emotions," (p.11). Consequently, social integration will become easier as skills are interfaced and organizational commitment become important to employees. The social integration will enmesh the efforts of individuals to make them productive employees to the organization. This means involvement, recognition, and acceptance of employees' contributions by employers as employees in turn support the organization's goals.

Reactive Emotional Responses

These usually negative emotions are associated with specific types of behaviours that occur spontaneously without much cognitive thought or concern for the consequences. People lose their cool and say things impulsively without concern or care for the outcome of their actions. Often, at the end of such outbursts an individual will make excuses and blame the weather, another person's action, or any circumstance that can take the responsibility for such behaviour.

Generally, patterns of unsociable behaviours relate to negative emotions. Those behaviours will influence any situation and turn it into conflict. Still, Parrott 2002, argued that "negative emotions can be useful and even desirable, and that emotional intelligence includes recognizing and exploiting this unity" (p.341). This is indeed arguable, but does not seem very improbable.

For instance, if someone receives an unfair appraisal more than once from the same supervisor, it is an opportunity for the recipient to appraise his skills and seek for alternative employment. This is even more so when there are no recourses because if the supervisor gets away with unfairness with no reprimand from the superiors, there is certainly no recourse. It would be advisable for the employee in this situation to move on to another job.

Still, it can turn out better for an individual if he has skills that are competitive and will land him into a better position elsewhere. Maybe, he would not have thought about leaving if everything was rosy with his supervisor and him.

Chapter 22   Conflict and the Workplace

Conflict is one of those situations that will meet us face-to-face on any given day, in a working environment. It is an integral factor in all of life's situations. Various types of disagreements between individuals can become destructive, resulting in loud hurtful words. Frequently, individuals allow feelings to dictate the way they should behave and this is where conflicts begin.

After an event occurs, the interface of cognitive, affective, and behaviour processes, often brings about a conflict situation. Usually it is not the event itself, which cause interpersonal conflict; but the way individuals interpret other people's behaviour, and the influence of the behaviour on their emotions.

However, when conflict is unresolved, it causes frustration, stress, and various types of emotional and psychological symptoms. The fact about conflict is that it is not always avoidable. The reason is that people are different, and no two persons *always* agree with each other *all* the time.

The presence of conflict is in all types of groups and relationships where people interact with one another. Consequently, there is no need for a scientific research to prove that the presence of conflict influence interpersonal relationships in a setting such as the workplace.

Although people often try to avoid interpersonal conflicts, this may only be an outward appearance; but on the inside, there is confusion, and turmoil and even a plan on how to get even with the one who has caused injury.

In the case of emotional abuse, the employee may seek out opportunities to sabotage equipment, or cause delays to important deadlines.

While this is factual, many times the avoidance of the existence of conflict, its denial, and repression creates a false impression, even when the atmosphere tells a different story.

It is in those situations that people will respond to conflict with outbursts of anger, display of poor interpersonal relationships, and poor communication with managers and other workers.

The consensus among researchers is that conflict of itself is innocuous.

Seemingly, what causes destructive behaviours in conflict situations, are the methods used for handling issues, and ignoring the presence of conflict by pretending that it does not exist.

Furthermore, according to Slaikeu & Hasson (1998) "the misguided use of four primary methods of conflict resolution – avoidance, collaboration, power plays, and higher authority – is what wastes money, kills business relationships, and in some cases results in the loss of life" (p.4).

Managers and supervisors are often the cause for conflict situations, which result in disastrous outcomes.

Occasionally, those outcomes are the result of an employee's evaluation from the immediate supervisor. The reason is that an unfair evaluation will cause the individual to express hostility in his/her behaviour when there is no recourse for remedy.

Conflict is Systematic

We can view conflict as being systematic or progressive because it always begins with one person who is frustrated, disgruntled, or dissatisfied about some type of issue, and this might affect others. After a hurtful event, the injured individual may take feelings to a height involving many more persons, and this gradually continues until the situation gets out of hand.

Moreover, that person may choose to respond immediately or decides to delay and thereby internalizes the situation and processes it through the thinking channels. While the process is going on, the thoughts are active with various ideas for response. Some are negative, others are positive. It is during that exercise the emotions become involved, and the individual looks at the event and attaches feelings to the encounter.

From those feelings, he generates behaviours, which will either escalate or de-escalate the situation. That person will decide how to confront the person who caused the injury. The confrontation will be either destructive or constructive, and may involve at least one other person, or other persons.

Evidently, conflict begins with an antecedent that has hurtful factors to create embarrassment, tension, humiliation or any kind of feelings, which will motivate an individual to take action in order for the feelings to subside.

Those uncomfortable feelings from the event can be guilt, sorrow, regret, sadness, defeat, or even helplessness. Those feelings are motivating factors to make the individual express emotions in an attempt to bring relief from pain. It is very important to express feelings because they are part of life and we cannot run away from them. However, there are ways to express feelings of hurt without making the situation worse. For example, look at the illustration below.

During the course of the morning, *A* used the copier. This does not mean that she was the last person to use it since there are six persons who have access to the machine. *B* comes to use it for a large project. She did not check the machine to find out what colour paper was in the tray. Instead, she placed a six-page document for ten copies each on the machine and left. Upon her return, she discovered that the copies were on coloured paper. *B* is very annoyed after a bad morning, and angrily walked over to *A* to confront her.

B: I have a word to say to you. Why did you not remove the coloured paper from the tray? Now after copying my project, I had to begin all over again.

Do you not think of other people other than yourself? What is wrong with you, do you not think? Do you need someone to tell you everything?

I am sick of your nonsense. You had better not do it again, otherwise; the supervisor will have to hear about this.

All that paper will be lost. She walks away just as angrily as she came. *A* is surprised and riled up…

Figure 5

A Systematic View of Conflict

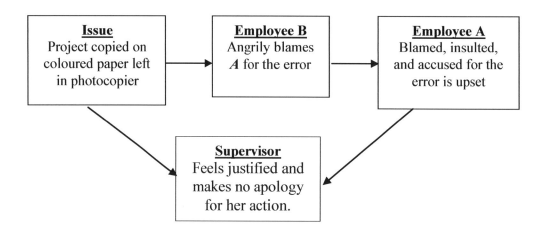

This is an illustration of unwarranted blame and accusation. *First*, B's approach was evidence of lack of professionalism and disrespect. *Second*, she did not ask any questions before assuming that A was the one responsible, even though there are six persons including herself and A, who use the machine.

Third, B issued a threat to A, promising to make a report to the supervisor. *Fourth*, it is clear that B is not in control of her emotions. *Fifth*, B projected her feelings on to A by insinuating that she is incompetent. In fact, one could easily say that B insulted A's intelligence. Eventually, both employees will be seeing the supervisor whichever way A responds to B's behaviour.

Conflict can be of Value

Despite the destructive nature of conflict, it can be functional when it "supports the goals of the group and improves its performance" (Robbins, 1991, p.430). Furthermore, constructive conflict management leads to successful personal achievement when goals are defined, and accomplished.

Individuals also learn active critical thinking, in terms of deductive reasoning in order to form inferences to arrive at conclusions. This activity stimulates creative problem solving that results in a higher quality of decision-making. Furthermore, in a group or organization the exercise will create great values that will strengthen relationships, act as a catalyst for change in policies, and enhance the development of effective problem solving and decision-making skills.

Additionally, values conflict will encourage each individual to listen to the other person and analyze different options to arrive at effective solution for problems. It means that each person will have an opportunity to speak freely without retribution or fear from others.

Conflict Empowers

When employees feel safe to voice their opinions in a warm climate, they will have no fear of expressing their views even in the presence of senior personnel. Moreover, they will also accept challenges to use skills that will engender harmony and camaraderie among each other. This will strengthen relationships so that they can all work towards one goal of achieving excellence and improved production for the organization or institution. However, empowerment only occurs when individuals have opportunities to be open, honest, and assertive in expressing feelings in a warm and non-threatening atmosphere.

Conflict can be Costly

Time

There are occasions when situations occur in the workplace causing valuable time to be lost to resolve disputes between workers, and between worker and managers. Without doubt, on any given day, there are dynamics, which are always present to cause conflict when individuals are in close proximity to one another. Interpersonal conflict only needs one other person to get the loop going to cause a systematic flow of events that will create a serious problem. For example, if one worker ignores the signal from the copier to re-fill the tray with paper, this alone can stimulate someone to say the wrong thing, and this creates a situation causing hurt feelings.

If this problem continues to smoulder, the result can be disastrous unless the persons involved spend time to talk about the situation often in the presence of a third person who has to listen, discuss, and find a way to resolve the issues. An exercise such as that takes valuable time.

Workplace conflict can become costly if there are no attempts to resolve issues in a timely fashion; or when uncomfortable situations are unresolved and left to ferment until someone decides to take action. For example, if there are bad feelings between the manager and an employee, this will create delays and even losses for the company.

If the feelings were due to the fact that the manager shouts at the employee this is a reflection of disrespect. No one appreciates being put-down or to be humiliated. One incident can take many hours to resolve while work is left undone, telephones are not answered, and in some cases people are kept waiting.

Finance

Many corporate organizations and institutions have paid out considerable sums of money because senior employees have abused their authority causing employees who have suffered emotional abuse to take legal actions. Moreover, "litigation expenses include attorney time for depositions, expert witnesses, trial preparations, trial, and appeal" (Slaikeu & Hasson, 1998, p.14).

One mistake from a manager, dean, professor, or supervisor can become very costly to the organization or institution because of their behaviours. Those behaviours could be emotional abuse from discrimination, unchecked prejudices, racism, and so on. If employers conduct regular checks on their managers and supervisors, they might save themselves from the high costs of litigations. Nonetheless, in some cases, there were reports made to higher authorities against supervisors and managers, but those reports were ignored, and the behaviours continued with no effort for change.

Often, after making the report, the employee who works with those persons is at their mercy for more emotional brutality with no recourse. There are times when the only outlet is to leave the place of employment after years of abusive treatment. It is from those situations that usually bring litigations against employers.

High turnover

Another reason for the high costs of workplace conflicts is the high turnover of staff. This means the hiring of new employees to fill vacant positions. The costs include advertisement, training, and over-work of those who have to carry on until the new person is hired. Sometimes, the employer has to hire temporary staff, which can be extremely costly to the company.

Conflict can be costly when emotions become the vehicle for expressing discontent, and cruel administrators ignore hurting people.

In one situation, the employee spent many years to obtain redress for the incompetence of insensitive supervisors. In the end, the individual was emotionally broken, and no compensation can repay the strain and emotional pain suffered while on the job and even after leaving the employment.

It came to the point where the person could not go near the workplace even to attend meetings to discuss the case. The effect of the experience was so traumatic that the individual had to be placed under long-term psychiatric care.

Workplace conflicts are dangerous when they become destructive and hurtful to the emotional health of employees. People become frustrated and tensed, making them angry and even fearful of the outcome of their grievances. This is where emotions and conflict interfaces.

Usually, the expressed emotions of the individuals are the only significant evidence that proves the presence of conflict. The environment becomes thick with resentment, frustrations, animosities, and hostilities.

Each person will face some degree of conflict on a daily basis, and the emotional experiences associated with the issues will influence performance. Those emotions will be expressed in either negative or positive behaviours.

Results of Emotional Conflicts

- Breakdown in communication and interpersonal relationships
- Absenteeism
- High turnover
- Poor performance
- Physical sickness
- Stress, frustration, depression, and anxiety
- Misunderstandings
- Miscommunications

Emotional and psychological abuse

- Low self-esteem
- Lack of self-confidence
- Fear
- Increased errors/mistakes
- Isolation
- Demoralization
- Panic
- Disrespect

Chapter 24   Factors Causing Workplace Conflicts

In order to understand how emotions influence conflict in the workplace it is important to have an understanding of the factors that create those problems. However, the emotional responses will depend on the nature of organizational events and the impact they have on the workers. Departmental or global re-organization activities can affect those closely connected to the factors that will bring about changes. Employees can become insecure when an organization decides to make changes. Furthermore, if employees receive *unkind* or *unfair remarks* from managers, they may have deepening effect on their *social*, *emotional*, and *psychological health*. Nonetheless, organizational changes are not the only factors that will cause workplace emotional conflicts. Other factors include:

Employee Unmet Needs

When emotions become the precursor to conflict, this can be the result of unmet needs – social, personal, or work-related situations such as abuse. It can also be the result of differences in personal interests, age, sex, ideals, inadequate equipment, tension, lack of resources and information. Other factors could be language, educational, and cultural differences that will create conflicting situations in the workplace. Conflict can arise out of those situations due to impatience and misunderstanding of the majority towards someone who is different in any of those situations.

Communication Problems

Moreover, workplace conflict can be the result of miscommunication, misconceptions, and incorrect assumptions about a group or an individual who is from a different culture. Such beliefs can result in stereotyping, prejudice, and discrimination. Conflict will occur in any situation where there are people with varying types of differences, and who are not willing to accept those who are different from they are. The influence of emotions on conflict is an ongoing process because of peoples' subjective feelings, their perception about events, and the interactions of cognitive, behavioural, and affective factors. For example, if an individual is upset about an abusive action from a superior or colleague against him, that might create outbursts of anger because after appraising the behaviour he feels hurt and believes that he was unjustly treated.

Personal Values

Emotions influence conflicts because of the perceptions of individuals facing workplace issues. Nevertheless, conflict is natural, inevitable, normal, and often necessary. Conflicts will reveal strengths and weaknesses in a department, among workers and managers. Conflicts can precede emotional events, and emotional events can precede conflicts. This all depends on each situation, the persons involved, their perceptions of the events, and experience. Most importantly, it also depends on whether those individuals are able to control their emotions. Obviously, the effective management of one's emotions is significant to the de-escalation of interpersonal conflict in a given situation. Here again, values and personality differences do play a major role even in the escalation or de-escalation of interpersonal conflict.

Employer Indifference to Problems

However, the existence of conflict is not the problem; but rather, it is the handling of a conflict situation that makes the difference. One reason why the presence of conflict would seem problematic is the way it might have been dealt with in the past. Still, various types of methods can be used to resolve conflicts. These include effective communication, negotiation, and mediation. In some situations, conflict can be over-simplified by distorting the nature and dynamics, or over-emphasized by placing too much attention to something that is minor. This depends on the perceptions of the disputants and the issues at stake. In some cases, employers willfully ignore issues by considering them unimportant, thus causing employee emotional distress, which might eventually escalate a conflict situation. If an employer constantly disregards an employee's plea for help, this indifference can turn out to be very costly. There are situations where employees have sued employers for emotional pain and suffering as the result of a supervisor's insensitive behaviours.

Unfair Performance Appraisal

One of the situations that will affect emotions is the threat of using performance appraisal to gain employees' compliance. Hence, an employee who has to suppress his/her feelings in the face of unfair treatment might do so to prevent getting a bad review. That person may silently become bitter and resentful. Instead of threatening an individual with a bad review, the insightful supervisor will try to help that person improve performance, adjust to the goals of the department, and change any negative behaviours are causing problems in the environment for a better working relationship.

Veiled Hints

A manager of a high-tech company reported that his CEO sent him an email with job listings outside of the company. This information was unsolicited by the employee, and he was extremely surprised by the chief's move. The individual took the matter seriously and considered the hint to be a dismissal. Of course, the matter was handled in a nonchalant manner as an error in judgment. Nothing more was said. In such a situation, any employee would feel uneasy not knowing the reason for the CEO's action. The employee took a proactive action and immediately found a better position with another company.

Personality Differences

No two persons are alike. Some individuals are extroverts while others are introverts and they each deal with their emotional events in different ways. I am almost convinced that some employers believe that everyone is the same and therefore must be treated as the next person. What makes matters worse is to note that the persons who make such errors in judgment are intellectuals with years of scholarly experience. Yet they do not acknowledge each human being as different from the other. Each individual was created uniquely, and no two persons are alike. It does not matter that individuals share ethnic, cultural, biological, geographical, or racial similarities. There are major differences even between twins. Therefore, employers ought to treat each person similar to the way they desire to be treated if the situation was changed. Still, when the differences of individuals are ridiculed, or disregarded such attitudes will influence the activity of emotional events resulting in emotional conflicts.

Employer's Expectations

Another perspective has to do with employers' expectations from an employee whether those expectations are explicitly detailed in the job descriptions or they are only implied. There are times when the misinterpretations of events set off a chain of emotional reaction affecting others, thus creating an environment of mistrust and interpersonal conflict. Conversely, the situation could be that the employee did not fulfill the obligations required and this too will cause friction and even termination. Despite all that, the employer may expect more from the employee than is reasonable causing the employee to become anxious and distressed.

Employee Unfulfilled Expectations

In contrast, the employee also has expectations and those, similar to the employers' are either explicit or implicit. Another situation concerning the influence on emotions and conflict in the workplace is the disappointment workers face after the "honeymoon period." Usually, at the bottom of the application form one reads "Equal Employee Opportunity" [EEO], meaning, anyone is free to apply regardless of colour, sex, age, or etc. However, many employees have learned that there are hidden elements not easily recognizable after the last handshake.

Frequently, it is after the period of probation that the real factors concerning the establishment and the job are exposed. Is it negligence on the employer's part for being mysterious about the true details of the job? Is the employer just being prudent because he has to meet legislative requirements?

The next question then is, "what does EEO means to the employee who has high expectations and discovers that he or she is barred from promotion in a particular department/division because of colour, age, or gender? These are questions, for which most employees who have experienced biases and hurt in the workplace are seeking answers. Occasionally, when expectations are unfulfilled, this leaves the wounded person with disappointment and resentment.

Environmental Stimuli

Emotional conflict can be reactions to the many types of stimuli that are in the environment. Those stimuli can, and do affect the individual psychologically, socially, and emotionally. The result includes anger, depression, stress, tension, withdrawal, and many other situations.

Research report states that, "peoples' experience and feelings influence and occasionally even determine the communicative behaviour and the course of conversations" (Fiehler, 2002, p.79). It is natural for people to respond to stimuli according to the way they understand and interpret them, and the way those situations affect them. Some people often mask their emotions and behave in a passive manner while others will be assertive, and or aggressive as a response to maltreatment.

Obviously, positive stimuli will result in favourable responses as opposed to those that are negative, and which cause frustration, hurt, and embarrassment. Another most important point is that people will choose to respond from their repertoire of learned behaviours or by spontaneity. In addition, the influence of environmental stimuli can be expressed directly or indirectly.

When environmental stimuli directly influence an organization to change its practices, social processes, or task design this can have a positive or negative outcome because the emotions are the reactions of the employees to the organizational events as they interpret them. Clearly then, the perception of the environment stimuli plays a vital role in the emotional response of employees to them.

Ostracism

An employee is sometimes excluded because of colour, age, language differences, or other factors. For example, some employees at the same levels are introduced to visitors while others are totally ignored. A manager who is hierarchical can stand in the way of his assistant. He does this by giving unfair appraisals so that the individual does not aspire any further than where he/she is in a department. These are evidences of workplace situations that can influence emotional conflicts because of their effect on interpersonal relationships amongst workers. Ostracism can be very subtle and therefore, hardly recognizable because the perpetrators usually display a false impression of being friendly and fair, thus deluding the unsuspecting target.

Emotional Blackmail

Since emotions are communication cues, it is possible that another person will work on an individual with his/her weakest emotion to evoke a reaction. For example, if by using the threat of giving a bad review to get an employee to do something that is against a moral value, clearly the employer is working on the employee's emotions.

Alienation

An employee is alienated or ostracized if that person has different moral, spiritual beliefs, or opinions from others. Also, gender and cultural differences can bring about alienation.

Verbal Assault

The abuser uses languages that are hurtful and demeaning to the other person. For example, "you are too sensitive." "You need to live and enjoy yourself. All that religion is no good." These also include, belittling, name-calling, blaming, criticizing, and other demeaning concepts.

Ignoring

Many employers do not validate their employees for their accomplishments. It is usual for an employee to improve himself educationally, only to be denied promotion or financial increase.

Some Reasons for Workplace Conflicts

1. *Close human interactions* – misunderstanding of communication cues, symbols

2. *Differences of opinions* - values, beliefs.

3. *Individual differences* – personalities, threats

4. *Managerial* – lacking leadership and interpersonal skills

5. *Cultural* – languages - mores, symbols

6. *Poor working environment* – physical, social, unfairness, job security

7. *Lack of opportunities* – promotion, job enrichment, job insecurity

8. *Lack of team integration* - unfairness, inequalities.

9. *Underemployment* - under-compensated

10. *Poor job selection* – incompatibility.

11. *Micro management* or too many bosses

12. *Lack of performance* - recognition.

13. *Overworked* – too many responsibilities

14. *Blame* – wrongful accusations, and unwarranted criticism

15. *Non-confrontational* – stork mentality, avoid, escape

16. *Misunderstanding of policies* – austere policies

Chapter 25   The Influence of Emotions on Conflict

There are many definitions given to conflict; but the one that will be used is "an expressed struggle between at least two interdependent parties who perceive incompatible goals, scarce resources, and interference from the other party in achieving their goals" (Hocker & Wilmot, 1991). This definition can be positioned at both employers and employees because they each have specific goals for which they need each other. The struggle occurs when differences occur, and there is evidence of dissatisfaction between the two groups. The dissatisfaction could be personality differences, discrimination, and disrespect on either side, or anything that might cause discomfort to the other. Emotions influence conflict in three particular areas cognitive, affective, and behavioural and they each interface with each other in a given situation. [See the diagram below].

Figure 6
The ABC of Conflict and Emotions
<u>Conflict and the Workplace</u>
<u>Interaction of Cognitive, Affective, and Behavioural Factors</u>

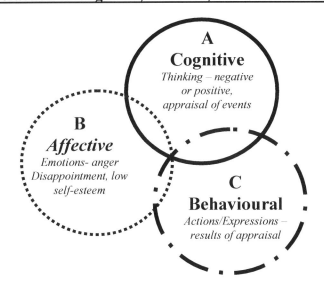

In the diagram above, when an incident takes place this affects the thinking process of the individual, the emotions, and eventually the behaviour. For example, a supervisor mistreats an assistant. The assistant believes the supervisor dislikes her. The assistant then displays behaviours that are uncaring and disrespectful. She might also behave in a subtle way by pretending that she is busy and does not hear when the supervisor speaks to her. She might also take a long time in the washroom or misplace files. The influence of emotions is an integral aspect of workplace conflicts.

Petra sat at her desk one morning, when the manager stood behind her while she works, making her nervous. Petra was quiet, and always avoided a fight, which made the manager upset. She made several private complaints against him, but was reluctant to bring the issue into the open.

The situation reported above revealed an atmosphere in which emotional abuse existed over a long period. That incident could not have been something that just happened. It had to have been a systematic behaviour by the manager, which got out of control when Petra confronted him. Professional bullies do not like confrontation by anyone who seems to disagree with them. In such a situation as Petra's, whether the nature of the emotional abuse is work-related stress on the manager's side or personal, quite likely there will be evidence of interpersonal conflicts. The reason is that emotions influence interpersonal relationships and is a conveyor of conflict situations.[x] Obviously, the behaviour of the manager must have created a hostile working environment for both Petra and any other workers in the vicinity.

Emotions influence interpersonal conflicts and this will make the environment become unfriendly, and unpleasant for workers. Our emotions are factors of our thinking and the way we feel. Therefore, our behaviours come from the combination of our thoughts and feelings. The nature of those actions can be sociable or unsociable, constructive or destructive.

Emotions influence our lives to make us act rationally or irrationally. In our rational state, we take time to think about consequences and the impact of an emotional outburst. While in our irrational state, we act impulsively, with anger and shouting and in some extreme cases become physical.

In addition, emotions influence our behaviours in a subjective manner because no matter how someone tells us that "everything will be all right" it does not change how we feel about an event. We will hold on to our feelings because they are real. It is from those feelings that we begin to think about how we will respond to an emotion.

Moreover, emotions will influence our lives when we develop unreasonably thoughts about an incident. For example, Jackie might think that Ronnie will give her an unfavourable review if she confronts him for blaming her without first being able to express her side of an incident.

106

In this type of situation, Jackie will make decisions that will either enhance her emotional health or gradually destroy it. Two major advantages of being able to confront a supervisor or employee about workplace issues, serves to alleviate tension, thereby de-escalate interpersonal conflicts. Those actions will result in a conducive and harmonious working environment.

However, when individuals are unable to make their feelings known, this only cause deeply entrenched resentment and produce bad attitudes among workers. Each one feels threatened either veiled or openly from the other. Since most attitudes are expressed in behaviours, the environment will be saturated with discontent and interpersonal conflicts. Workers will feel insecure and there will be a lack of trust and loyalty among them.

Researches have been carried out concerning the influence of emotions in the workplace relating to emotional labour and emotional intelligence.[xi] If employees have to respond to infractions from other employees, clients, or students with a prescribed script from the administrators, the suppression of their emotions will create intra-psychic conflict.

After a while that individual will begin to express symptoms from the internal feelings in the behaviour. There are times when we can adjust to a situation, but how long can any person continue working under superficiality and pretense.

Perception of an Emotion

Unmistakably, the awareness, relatedness, and the effect of an emotion are variables to evoke the decision for taking action after thinking about a painful situation. Seemingly, the understanding of an emotion will influence the individual to evaluate and appraise an event. Therefore, the outcome of the assessment will be the deciding factor about how to deal with a situation, and whether to confront or not to confront.

Evidently, in order to process emotional skills accurately and efficiently, one must understand one's own emotions with the insight to use them skillfully in problem solving (Tugade & Fredickson, 2002, p.319). The assumption is that people will respond to an emotional event according to their perception and interpretation after they have cognitively appraised the situation. The individual who responds to an emotional event subjectively thinks about the way he feels, and then appraises the event to see if he should take an aversive action or ignore the situation.

Averill (1994) affirmed that, "emotional feelings are often described as subjective as opposed to objective." Obviously, the outcome of the appraisal of an event will influence the offended person to make the decision for a positive evaluation. A positive result will lead to a proactive response that guides the individual to confrontation and collaborative discussion.

In contrast, the interpretation of the emotional event can also lead to a negative reaction to escalate conflict. This will inhibit interpersonal relationships, thus limiting group cohesion and efficiency (Ayoko & Härtel 2002, p.80). In addition, emotions can become evident with display of resentment, anger, bitterness, and frustration (p.91).

For instance, when an employee experience unfair treatment, there is the likelihood that feelings of dissatisfaction will be demonstrated in the behaviours. The reason is that, the cognitive influence of emotions and their interaction with behaviour will make the individual process an emotional event. According to his understanding of that event, he will be motivated to react towards the perpetrator.

After appraising the event, it is the *thought* [cognitive] of being mistreated that makes the individual *feels* badly [affective], and *acts* [behaviour] in a manner to satisfy the emotion being felt.[xii] In such a situation, the individual is acting subjectively, which is a feature of emotions. There are times when dissatisfaction is displayed with the use of cues such as facial expressions, voice inflection, verbal, or physical action (Feldman & Salovey, 2002).

Behavioural Expressions

Since "emotions involve feelings and experience; physiology and behaviour; cognitions and conceptualizations" (Ortony, Clore, & Collins, 1998, p.1; Parrott, 2002, p.344), evidently those feelings will be expressed in some form of behaviour. For example, if someone is excited this is seen in his face and body. There are smiles, and changes in the individual's position. Similarly, if that person is sad, he might become angry or show his feelings with raised eyebrows, lowered shoulders, or a frown on his face. Moreover, emotions are also evidenced in language, rage, and facial expressions.

Besides, an emotion can be expressed in a variety of ways. In the example in figure 1 with the assistant being treated unfairly, he might express his emotions after the event by being angry or by confronting the supervisor letting him know that he felt "upset," "uneasy", "insignificant," "devalued," or "inferior" to that kind of treatment. These concepts are emotional types (Ortony, Clore & Collins, 1998) that the individual might use to euphemize the way he felt to avoid bluntness that could lead to further conflict. Descriptions are carefully chosen to alleviate the impact a harsh word would otherwise have had on another individual.

Ortony, Clore, & Collins (1998) identified variables that affect the intensity of some emotions but not others. The researchers noted that

> Among the variables that affect the intensity of different emotions, are global which affect all emotions, and local variables, which affect particular groups of emotions. Global emotions variables include the *sense of reality*, i.e., how much one believes the emotion-inducing situations is real; *proximity*, which depends on how close in psychological space one feels to the situation;

unexpectedness, which depends on how surprised one is by the situation; and *arousal*, which depends on how much one is aroused prior to the situation (pp.83-84).

Cognitive Process of Emotional Event

The angry response from the assistant in the example above is the result of his appraisal of the event. The response validates the point that events provoke emotions, after cognitive evaluation. Moreover, it is possible that the emotional arousal can interfere with performance, taking precedence above cognitive and social processes (Grandey & Brauburger, 2002, p.273, (cited Fiske & Taylor, 1991); Isen & Baron, 1991; Weiss & Corpanzano, 1996). Therefore, an individual can respond to an emotional event without thinking about the type of response that he will give. An action in this case would be impulsive if there was no thought concerning the effect or consequence of the response.

One example of this could be when someone makes an irrational statement at the wrong time that embarrasses another individual. After realizing his action, the individual apologizes "Oh, I don't know what came over me. I was not thinking. I am sorry." The quick remorse might save the moment, but the injured person might place the incident into his collection of hurts to use against the individual in another situation. The parties might have been a subordinate and a supervisor. Managers and supervisors have kept scores of occasional slight infractions by employees that usually appear at year-end reviews.

Situations such as a client making a remark unknowingly against an employee will become the deciding factor whether there will be an increment or a promotion. Employees have reported that they knew nothing of those incidents until when receiving their reviews. This type of managing is injurious to the employee, and it will stimulate emotions that will lead to interpersonal conflicts.

Emotional Conflict Case Study
Supervisor and Assistant

Susan and Jim are ready for the start of a three-day training workshop. There are at least twenty persons milling around waiting for the trainer. In the midst of this, there was a small group close by. The vendor came with the refreshment, invoice signed, and left. Jim checked off the items and discovered that there were a few things missing from the list. It was his fault since he had given Susan the list with the items that he wanted. Immediately, without thinking Jim pounced on Susan in the presence of the small group of about five persons who were close by, and stated, *"You don't ever, follow instructions. I just can't trust you to do anything right."*

Obviously, the statement was a direct attack on Susan. She felt humiliated because people were looking and most of them heard what Jim said because he did not try to muffle his voice. Although she tried to maintain her composure, which she was not doing well at that moment, the group could see that she was upset. Susan was very angry and would have said something, but decided against doing so. She walked out angrily, without responding to Jim.

Analysis of Event

1. Reflect on the statement and describe your perceptions – sensitivity, timing, tone, and respect.

2. If you were in the place of the assistant, how would you have felt?

3. Where was Susan when the statement was made?

4. What effect the presence of the group had on Susan's emotions?

5. What are the emotions detected in the statement?

6. Describe the quality of relationship between Jim and Susan.

7. What concepts could you elicit from the statement that would escalate conflict? For example, blame, or sarcasm.

8. Can you point out the main *stingers* in the statement?

<u>Figure 7</u>
Case Study 2
Emotional Conflict
Supervisor and Assistant

1 **Event** *Verbal attack* **J.** *(You do not follow instructions. I just can't trust you to do anything right)*.	**2** **Perception** *[Awareness]* **S**. *Surprised, evaluates the statement.* **Why is he blaming me?**
3 **Cognitive** *[Appraisal]* S: **He thinks that I am incompetent. I will not take this from him**. *[Outcome of the evaluation]*.	**4** **Emotion** *[Feelings]* S: **She is very angry.**

5

Behaviour
[Action]
S. *Walks out of the workshop*

©2013 Diagram Adapted by B. Y. Stuart

112

Figure 8
The ABC of Conflict
Showing the Interface of Affective, Behavioural, and Cognitive Processes

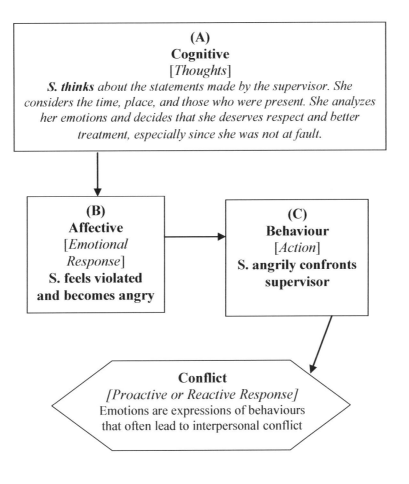

(A)
Cognitive
[*Thoughts*]
S. thinks *about the statements made by the supervisor. She considers the time, place, and those who were present. She analyzes her emotions and decides that she deserves respect and better treatment, especially since she was not at fault.*

(B)
Affective
[*Emotional Response*]
S. feels violated and becomes angry

(C)
Behaviour
[*Action*]
S. angrily confronts supervisor

Conflict
[Proactive or Reactive Response]
Emotions are expressions of behaviours that often lead to interpersonal conflict

113

Table 4
Analysis of Emotional Event
An Assumption of the Event with Jim and Susan

Cognitive Evaluation:
Susan (thoughts) - "He disrespected me in the presence of all those people, and intimated that I was *incompetent*."
What will S do now? Ignore the remark; be reactive or proactive.

Psychological Outcome:
- She was distressed, angry, anxious, frustrated, irritated.
- *Should she take out her frustration on others or seek for some way, to confront Jim?*
- *Should she keep quiet and not refer to the incident?*

Physiological outcome:
- Facial expression [raised eyebrows]
- Change in voice inflection – tone
- Withdrawal
- Increased heartbeat

Behavioural Expressions:
- Anger
- Avoidance
- Escape
- Shrugged shoulders
- Walked out

Should Susan behave in a manner for everyone to see that she had been offended?

Copyright ©Diagram Adapted by B. Y. Stuart 2013

Chapter 26   Problem Solving

One of the most important factors that will create a healthy working environment is the ability to problem solve in conflict situations. Despite this ideal, there are people who possess those skills in a pedagogical setting, but lack the practical application in demonstrating them in a conflict situation. Observably, those individuals seem unable to control their emotions in a conflict setting.

However, emotions can be controlled in a conflict situation, but they should not be suppressed. If the individual is angry then nothing is wrong with such feelings so long as they do not turn out to be vindictive and hostile leading to destructive behaviours. Those negative responses will cause conflict to escalate and create communication breakdown and influence workplace conflicts.

The mistake some individuals make is "distancing oneself from the distressing meaning of a situation" (Lazarus & Lazarus, (1994) p.164), which will eventually escalate the conflicting problem because they are not being resolved. It is true that one can be distanced from a destructive situation by not assimilating it, but if that individual has to work within the environment, it can later affect his health.

Lazarus & Lazarus further noted that, "people cope with stressful situations in ways that are damaging to health" (p.255). Consequently, when conflict is not resolved with the appropriate problem-solving skills, this can lead to poor communication and the breakdown of interpersonal relationships

Dealing with Emotionally Induced Conflict
The resolution of conflict situations must be in a controlled, non-threatening, and warm climate to evoke understanding and respect. The facilitator must be able to communicate congruently with effective listening skills and positive body language as well as verbal. The body language tells the speaker if the listener is present. Another way of detecting whether the listener is paying attention reflects on the types of questions asked. By asking open-ended questions, for clarification, explanation, and understanding show that the listener is attentive.

In addition, being reflective is also extremely vital because the listener is able to empathize with feelings to the other person. Empathy means that he is putting himself in the other person's shoe in an attempt to see the issues from their perspectives. Moreover, it means that there is compassion, thoughtfulness for each person, with appreciation and full support. It is also essential that each party in the dispute receives equal treatment.

The listener must endeavour to stress the desire to have the conflict resolved in an amicable manner, even if all the needs cannot be met. Nonetheless, every attempt must be made to reach a consensus where each party is satisfied with the outcome because this would be a significant step into the right direction.

It is important that the listener follows the ground rules and respect moments of silence. He should find out what the conflict is about and deal with the issues by identifying interests and positions. No attack should be made on the persons or their culture.

The avenues are arbitration, litigation, mediation, and negotiation. The listener can help the parties decide on which method to choose for resolution.

It is important to pay special attention to factors such as costs and time and the outcome each party desires.

Despite which method is used, when there is a problem resulting in conflict it should not be ignored because this will prolong the conflict. Emotions must be acknowledged and dealt with. Otherwise, they will impinge on the communication process and the management of conflict.

For example, the individual might be aggressive, passive, or assertive. In any case, not all emotions are destructive and further, they can add to the successful outcome of problem solving. This is especially so when employees know that they are being appreciated, and there are genuine feelings of empathy on the part of a supervisor towards them.

References

Averill, J.R. (1994). I Feel, Therefore I am – I Think. In The Nature of Emotion: Fundamental Questions. Ekman, P. & Davidson, R.J. (Eds.), pp. 379-393. Oxford University Press.

Ayoko, O.B. & Härtel, C.E.J. (2002). The Role of Emotion and Emotion Management in Destructive and Productive Conflict in Culturally Heterogeneous Work Groups. In Managing Emotions in the Workplace. Ashkanasy, N.M., Zerbe, W.J., & Härtel, C.E.J. (Eds.), pp.77-97. M.E. Sharpe, Publishers.

Andersen, P.A. & Guerrero, L.K. (1998). Principles of Communication and Emotion in Social Interaction. In Handbook of Communication and Emotion: Research, Theory, Applications, and Concepts. Andersen, P.A., & Guerrero, L.K. (Eds.), pp. 49-96. Academic Press.

Bassman, E.S. (1992). Abuse in the Workplace: Management Remedies and Bottom Line Impact. Quorum Books.

Beehr, T.A. (1995). Psychological Stress in the Workplace. Routledge.

Bramson, R.M., (1981). Coping With Difficult People. Anchor Press Edition.

Buller, D.B. & Burgoon, J.K. (1998). Emotional Expression in the Deception Process. In Handbook of Communication and Emotion: Research, Theory, Applications, and Concepts. Andersen, P.A., & Guerrero, L.K. (Eds.), pp. 381-402. Academic Press.

Caruso, D.R., & Wolfe, C.J. (2001). Emotional Intelligence in the Workplace. In Emotional Intelligence in Everyday Life: A Scientific Inquiry. Ciarrochi, J., Forgas, J.P., & Mayer, J.D. [Eds.], pp. 150-167. Psychology Press, Taylor & Francis Group.

Clore, G.C. (1994). Why Emotions are Felt. In The Nature of Emotion: Fundamental Questions. Ekman, P. & Davidson, R.J. (Eds.), pp. 103-111. Oxford University Press.

Coyne, J. (2001). Mood and Persuasion: A Cognitive Response Analysis. In Emotions in Social Psychology. Parrott, W.G. (Ed.). (p. 227). Taylor & Francis Press.

Effenbein, H.A., Marsh, A.A., & Ambudy, N.(2003). Emotional Intelligence and the Recognition of Emotion from Facial Expression. In The Wisdom in Feeling: Psychological Processes in Emotional Intelligence. Barrett, L.F. & Salovey, P. (Eds.), pp.37-59. Guildford Press.

Ekman P., Friesen, V., & Arcoli, S. (2001). Facial Signs of Emotional Experience. In Emotions in Social Psychology. Parrott, W.G. (Ed.), p. 255. Taylor & Francis Press.

Fiehler, R. (2002). How to do Emotions with words: Emotionality in conversations. In The Verbal Communication of Emotions: Interdisciplinary Perspectives. S.R. Fussell (Ed.), pp.79-106. Lawrence Erlbaum Associates, Publishers.

Forgas, J. & Bower, G.H. (2001). Mood Effects on Person-Perception Judgments. In Emotions in Social Psychology. Parrott, W.G. (Ed.), pp. 204-215. Taylor & Francis Press.

Goldie, P. & Spicer, F. (2002). In Understanding Emotions: Mind and Moral. Goldie, P. [Ed.]. Aldershot Publishing.

Grandey, A.A. & Brauburger, A.L. (2002). The Emotion Regulation Behind the Customer Service Smile. In Emotions in the Workplace: Understanding the Structure and Role of Emotions in Organizational Behaviour, pp. 273-275. Lord, R.G. Klimoski, R.J. & Kanfer, R. (Eds.). Jossey-Bass.

Gross, J.J. & John, O.P. (2002). Wise Emotion Regulations. In The Wisdom in Feeling: Psychological Processes in Emotional Intelligence. Barrett, L.F. & Salovey, P. (Eds.), pp. 297-318. Guildford Press.

Guerrero, L.K., Andersen, P.A., & Trost, M.R. (1998). Communication and Emotion: Basic Concepts and Approaches. In Handbook of Communication and Emotion: Research, Theory, Applications, and Concepts. Andersen, P.A., & Guerrero, L.K. (Eds.), pp. 3-27. Academic Press.

Hegtvedt, K.A. (1990). The Effects of Relationship Structure on Emotional Responses to Inequity. *Social Psychology Quarterly*, 53, (3), pp. 214-228.

Heise, D.R. & Calhan, C. (1995). Emotion Norms in Interpersonal Events. *Social Psychology Quarterly*, 58, (4), pp. 223-240.

Hibbert, A.L. (2002). Accepting Yourself. Writers Club Press an imprint of iUniverse, Inc.

Hochschild, A.R. (1983). The Managed Heart: Commercialization of Human Feeling. University of California Press.

Hocker, J.L. & Wilmot, W.W. (1991). Interpersonal Conflict. Dubuque, IA: William C. Brown.

Johnson, C., Ford, R., & Kaufman, J. (2000). Emotional Reactions to Conflict: Do Dependence and Legitimacy Matter? *Social Forces*, 79, (1), pp. 107-137.

Kruml, S.M. & Geddes, D. (2000). Catching Fire Without Burning Out! Is there an Ideal Way to Perform Emotional Labor? In Managing Emotions in the Workplace. Ashkanasy, N.M., Zerbe, W.J., & Härtel, C.E.J. (Eds.), pp.177-188. M.E. Sharpe, Publishers.

Lazarus, R.S. & Lazarus, B.N. (1994). Passion and Reason: Making Sense of Our Emotions. Oxford University Press.

Levenson, R.W. (1994,). Emotional Control: Variation and Consequences. In The Nature of Emotion: Fundamental Questions, pp. 272-279. Ekman, P. & Davidson, R.J. (Eds.), Oxford University.

Ledoux, J.E. (1994). The Degree of Emotional Control Depends on the Kind of Response System Involved. In The Nature of Emotion: Fundamental Questions, pp. 270-272. Ekman, P. & Davidson, R.J. (Eds.), Oxford University.

Lord, R.G. & Kanfer, R. (2002). Emotions and Organizational Behaviour. In Emotions in the Workplace: Understanding the Structure and Role of Emotions in Organizational Behaviour, pp. 10-11. Lord, R.G., Klimoski, R.J. & Kanfer, R. (Eds.), Jossey-Bass.

Lucas, J.W. 1999). Behavioural and Emotional Outcomes of Leadership in Task Groups. *Social Forces*, 78, (2), pp. 747-778.

MacDermid, S.M., Seery, B.L. & Weiss, H.M. (2002). An Emotional Examination of the Work-Family Interface. In Emotions in the Workplace: Understanding the Structure and Role of Emotions in Organizational Behaviour. Lord, R.G. Klimoski, R.J. & Kanfer, R. (Eds.), p.107. Jossey-Bass.

Manning, G. K. Curtis, & S. McMillen (1996). Building Community: The Human Side of Work. Thomson Executive Press.

Matthew, G., Zeidner, M., & Roberts, R.D. (2002). Emotional Intelligence: Science and Myth. MIT Press, Cambridge, MA.

Narramore, C.M. (1960). The Psychology of Counseling. Zondervan Publishing House.

Ortony, A., Clore, G.L., & Collins, A. (1988). The Cognitive Structure of Emotions. Cambridge University Press.

Parrott, W.G. (2002). The Functional Utility of Negative Emotions. In The Wisdom of Feeling: Psychological Processes in Emotional Intelligence. Barrett, L.F. & Salovey, P. (Eds.), pp. 341-359. Guildford Press.

Planalp, S. (1999). Communicating Emotions: Social, Moral, and Cultural Processes. Cambridge University.

Rimé, B., Corsini, S., & Herbette, G. (2002). Emotion, Verbal Expression, and the Social Sharing of Emotion. In The Verbal Communication of Emotions: Interdisciplinary Perspectives. S.R. Fussell (Ed.), pp.185-208. Lawrence Erlbaum Associates, Publishers.

Robbins, S.P. (1991). Organizational Behaviour: Concepts, Controversies, and Applications (Fifth Ed.). Prentice Hall International Editions.

Salovey, P., Hsee, C.K., & Mayer, J.D. (2001). Emotional Intelligence and the Self-Regulation of Affect. In Emotions in Social Psychology. Parrott, W.G. (Ed.), pp. 185-197. Taylor & Francis Press.

Sarason, I.G., & Sarason B.R. (1996). Abnormal Psychology: The problem of maladaptive behaviour. (8th edition). Prentice Hall.

Schachter, S. & Singer, J.E. (2001). Cognitive, Social, and Physiological Determinants of Emotional State. In Emotions in Social Psychology. Parrott, W.G. (Ed.), pp. 76-93. Taylor & Francis Press.

Slaikeu, K.A. & R.H. Hasson. (1998). Controlling The Costs of Conflict: How to Design a System for your Organization. Josey-Bass Publishers.

Smith, B.C. (2002. Keeping Emotions in Mind. In Understanding Emotions: Mind and Moral, pp. 111-121. Goldie, P. [Ed.]. Aldershot Publishing Company.

Stocker, M. (2002). Does being good means that you have the right emotions? In Understanding Emotions: Mind and Moral, pp. 66-79. Goldie, P. [Ed.]. Aldershot Publishing Company.

Tugade, M.M. & Fredrickson, B.L. (2002). Positive Emotions and Emotional Intelligence. In The Wisdom in Feeling: Psychological Processes in Emotional Intelligence. Barrett, L.F. & Salovey, P. (Eds.), pp. 319-340. Guildford Press.

Wharton, A.S. & Erickson, R.J. (1993). Managing Emotions on the Job and at Home: Understanding the Consequences of Multiple Emotional Roles. *Academy of Management Review*, 18, (3), pp. 457-486.

Wollheim, R. (1999). On the Emotions. Yale University.

Zerbe, W.J., Härtel, C.E.J & Ashkanasy, N.M. (2002). Emotional Labor and the Design of Work. In Managing Emotions in the Workplace. M.E. Sharpe, Publishers: pp. 276-296.

Zerbe, W.J., Härtel, C.E.J. & Ashkanasy, N.M. (2002). Emotional Labor and the Design of work. In Managing Emotions in the Workplace. Ashkanasy, N.M., Zerbe, W.J., & Hätel, C.E.J. (Eds.), pp. 276-296. M.E. Sharpe, Publishers.

Endnotes

[i] Hochschild, "An emotion is a biologically given sense, and our most important one" (p.219). She continued: "like other senses – hearing, touch, and smell, it is a means by which we know about our relations to the world, and it is therefore crucial for the survival of human beings in group life" (1983, p.3).

[ii] According to Bassman (1999) "Although employee abuse is not new, "it has taken a new feature with an environment of unending and relentless pressure due to increased competition and ineffective strategies for increasing competitiveness" (p.4).

[iii] Sarason & Sarason (1996) stated that, "a person's vulnerability to stress is influenced by his or her temperament, coping skills, and the available social support" (p.128).

[iv] Bramson, (1981) noted that "We have all learned more than one way to cope with threatening situations....most people tend to use one strategy at a time. If the first doesn't work,, that is, if the threat and conflict don't go away, then a second strategy is brought to bear" (p.200.

[v] Robbins, identified three sets of factors for potential sources of stress. They include environmental, organizational, and individual (1991).

[vi] Emotions have also been described as: "complex reactions that engage both our minds and our behaviours, thus making them cognitive and behavioural, psychological and physiological" (Lazarus & Lazarus, 1994, p.151; Buller & Burgoon, 1998, pp.382 & 383; Guerrero, Andersen, & Trost, 1998, p.7).

[vii] "The primary function of emotions and their expressions is to minimize rejection by other humans" (Anderson & Guerrero, 1998, p.51). Furthermore, "emotions evolved not just as internal control mechanisms, but as relatively universal communication systems that promote the group survival of humans" (p.50). This means that they are the main basis for information to others.

[viii] See Ortony, Clore & Collins (1998), for Emotion Type.

[ix] Planalp (1999) "emotions must be expressed and communicated" (p.111).

[x] "It is the emotional experience and expression that form part of our thoughts, feelings, and behaviours and they blend together to characterize the tapestry of interpersonal interaction" (Guerrero, Anderson, & Trost, 1998, pp.3-4).

[xi] Hochschild, researched emotional labor in various aspects of job situations in the workplace relating to flight attendants and bill collectors (1983).

In addition, quite a number of studies have focused on emotional intelligence (Effenbein, Marsh, & Ambudy, 2003; Matthew, Zeidner & Roberts, 2002; Tugade & Fredickson, 2002; Caruso & Wolfe, 2001).

[xii] "In most cases there is a good deal of agreement between a person's way of thinking and the emotions that person feels" (Parrott, 2002, p.10).

Made in the USA
Charleston, SC
03 May 2013